generation entrepreneur

- shape today's business reality
- create tomorrow's wealth
- do your own thing

books for the future minded

Welcome to the next generation of business.

There is a new world which we can look at but we cannot see. Yet within it, the forces of technology and imagination are overturning the way we work and the way we do business. ft.com books are both gateway and guide to this world. We understand it because we are part of it. But we also understand the needs of businesses which are taking their first steps into it, and those still standing hesitantly on the threshold. Above all, we understand that, as with all business challenges, the key to success lies not with the technology itself, but with the people who must use it and manage it. People like you; the future minded.

See a world of business.
Visit www.ft.com today.

Stuart Crainer & Des Dearlove

generation entrepreneur

- shape today's business reality
- create tomorrow's wealth
- do your own thing

FT.com
FINANCIAL TIMES

books for the future minded

An imprint of Pearson Education

London • New York • San Francisco • Toronto • Sydney • Tokyo • Singapore
Hong Kong • Cape Town • Madrid • Amsterdam • Munich • Paris • Milan

PEARSON EDUCATION LIMITED

Head Office:
Edinburgh Gate
Harlow CM20 2JE
Tel: +44 (0)1279 623623
Fax: +44 (0)1279 431059

London Office:
128 Long Acre
London WC2E 9AN
Tel: +44 (0)20 7447 2000
Fax: +44 (0)20 7240 5771
Website: www.business-minds.com

First published in Great Britain in 2000

© Pearson Education Limited 2000

The right of Stuart Crainer and Des Dearlove to be identified as Authors
of this Work has been asserted by them in accordance
with the Copyright, Designs and Patents Act 1988.

ISBN 0 273 64920 5

British Library Cataloguing in Publication Data
A CIP catalogue record for this book can be obtained from the British Library.

10 9 8 7 6 5 4 3 2

Typeset by Northern Phototypesetting Co. Ltd, Bolton
Printed and bound in Great Britain by Biddles Ltd, Guildford & King's Lynn

The Publishers' policy is to use paper manufactured from sustainable forests.

Contents

Acknowledgments   xi

Part 1

gen e   1

1   e world   3

Welcome to generation entrepreneur

2   from raising hell to raising capital   11

Forget the rebellious whirlwind of youth. Forget James Dean; think

James Lavelle

3   the bagel queen   15

From Salomon Brothers to bagels: pure gen e

4   e isn't x   19

Labels suck. Why gen e is not Generation X

5   dollars and amazonians   23

gen e superhero Jeff Bezos takes a bow

Part 2

defining a generation   27

6   a little bit hyperkinetic   29

e = energy. Only the restless need apply

7 united distillers 33

e = essence. gen e distil things down; and then do it again

8 only connect 37

e = electronic. Technology is only as good as the uses to which it is put

9 trained to the max 41

e = educated. gen e learn new tricks all the time

10 the calling 45

e = enthusiasm. gen e love their jobs. Business is a calling

11 people people 51

e = empathy. Business really is about people

12 emotional economics 53

e = emotion. Tapping into emotions is the new imperative

13 making a difference 57

e = ethics. Money only gets you so far

14 the ad men 65

Ethical ad men? Surely not

15 direct action 69

Cafédirect proves there is an awful lot of ethics in coffee beans

16 the art of balance 73

e = equilibrium. Making a million and blowing out the kids' birthday candles

17 cake eating 77

We want it all and we want it now. Dual careering

18 back to the lab 81

e = experimentation. Who said getting it wrong was a bad idea?

19 **persistence sucks** 85

James Dyson reinvents the vacuum cleaner

Part 3

the new economy 89

20 **the chicken and e** 91

The new economy is driven by entrepreneurs not technology

21 **sitting comfortably** 95

Sofabeds online? That'll be gen e

22 **the new economy is here to stay** 99

The bubble only inflates stock prices

23 **the Dell model** 101

Proof: a business model for our times

24 **beyond Silicon Valley** 107

Palo Alto doesn't have a monopoly on sunshine or innovation

25 **e hotbeds** 113

gen e take over the world

Part 4

power shifts 119

26 **brawn to brain** 121

Intellects really are the new capital

27 **thinkers for the new age** 125

New economy; new gurus

28 executive gold 131
Executive talent is in short supply

29 attracting gen e 137
Why should I work for you?

30 the new power elite 141
The talented can hold the corporate world to ransom

31 what if? 145
Innovation exemplars

32 outsider's paradise 149
Opinionated and troublesome, lone voices can change history

33 the beauty of virginity 155
Arise, Sir Richard of gen e

Part 5

e working 159

34 free at last 161
Free agents of the world unite

35 pez heads 165
Anyone for eBay?

36 e careers 169
Make it up as you go along

37 the richer the better 173
Julian Richer sounds for our times

38 taking control 179

The brand is you

39 the trouble with employability 187

One hand clapping or an ovation?

Part 6

corporate life and death 191

40 e inc 193

The same but different

41 organizational glue 201

The twenty-first-century corporation needs to be into industrial-strength adhesive

42 the loyalty factor 207

Loyalty lives on, but to what?

43 managing gen e 217

They still have to be managed

44 the value-led corporation 223

Values are the new dollar bills

45 managing with values 229

Malden Mills ignites the values debate

46 watch Bill 235

gen e started with Bill Gates. He is still doing quite well for himself, but for how long?

47   e pig 239

Mere mortals can turn gen e values to organizational advantage. New Pig
Corporation proves it

Notes   245

e info   251

Index   253

Acknowledgments

Every great contemporary endeavour has a man or woman in combat trousers behind it. In the case of *generation entrepreneur* that man was Richard Stagg of Pearson Education. Richard is the original cool hunter and we are grateful for his stream of newspaper cuttings, insights, and opinions, as well as his friendship.

We are also indebted to the various people we talked to and interviewed in writing the book. In addition, Kjell Nordström and Jonas Ridderstråle provided funky inspiration; Gerry Griffin was a constant source of distractions (and the material on power) and our colleague at Suntop Media, Georgina Peters, a steadying influence. Against the odds, Ro and Sara kept us in touch with reality.

Part 1

gen e

e world

'Thirty years ago MBA students dreamed of running General Motors; ten years ago they dreamed of working at Goldman Sachs; five years ago it was McKinsey. Now they dream about running their own company,' Antonio Borges, dean of the leading European business school INSEAD, told us.[1] There was nothing dreamy in his manner, no wistfulness for a departing era. Dean Borges is not the wistful type. This, looking out over the forest of Fontainebleau on a Fall evening in 1999, was a simple statement of reality.

Dean Borges is right. This is the era of the entrepreneur. What began in the entrepreneurial melting pot of Silicon Valley as a dream for a select few has become a worldwide phenomenon. For growing numbers of young people, creating a business has become a calling; a vocation; a mission. It is the spirit of the age. The new zeitgeist.

This is an age of individual aspiration. We want. We need. We demand. We clamour. On Maslow's hierarchy of needs we're off the scale. Sure, it's about making money, but it is also about making a mark. The new breed of entrepreneurs think differently about life in general – and business in particular. The new business

> This is an age of individual aspiration. We want. We need. We demand. We clamor. On Maslow's hierarchy of needs we're off the scale

breed are unlike anything that came before. Around the world, business is being democratized. People are standing on top of the managerial equivalent of the Berlin Wall with their arms raised in triumph. Entrepreneurs *über alles*.

The men and women who are the new wealth creators and shapers of business are generation entrepreneur. Corporate man and woman died out in the downsizing age. Yuppies look Neanderthal by comparison. Gen e are running the show now – and they are making up the rules as they go along. (As Indiana Jones said when asked what his plan was: 'I don't know; I'm making this up as I go.')

The change is evident even to the naked eye. In business, grey hair and conservative suits used to be compulsory. Tidy constraint was the order of the corporate day. (Think of the tie – an expression of membership, a fashion accessory – and the first thing removed from prisoners, not just to prevent suicide but to emasculate, remove a sense of belonging. Without a tie you are naked, tribeless.) Now fresh-faced entrepreneurs in combat pants stare out from countless business magazines. They do not wear ties. They have no need to belong.

In traditional corporate terms, some are just out of diapers. An American venture capitalist relates that a celebration dinner for a new company in Boston lacked fizz because the venture capitalists were the only ones at the table old enough to drink.[3] Forget reengineering and total quality management, youth is the new business wonder drug and Wall Street is tripping on it. Others are already hopelessly addicted. Venture capitalists now routinely – seemingly blindly at times – invest millions of dollars in an idea dreamed up by teenagers playing on a computer in a garage.

Some 46 per cent of businesses in America are now started by people who are 35 or under.[4] Them and us used to refer to workers and managers. Now it refers to the older generation of managers and their younger colleagues. The youth have it. And the old are making desperate attempts to catch up or get up to speed

---

> Gen e are running the show now – and they are making up the rules as they go along

> Now fresh-faced entrepreneurs in combat pants stare out from countless business magazines. They do not wear ties. They have no need to belong

| Table 1.1 | Wizards of e^2 | | | | |

Name	Age	Fact	Company	Title	Estimated wealth*
Michael Dell	34	College drop-out	Dell Computer	Chairman and CEO	$21.49 billion
Jeff Bezos	35	Princeton graduate	Amazon.com	CEO and chairman	$5.75 billion
Ted Waitt	36	Son of a cattle broker	Gateway	Chairman CEO	$5.44 billion
Pierre Omidyar	32	Bachelors from Tufts University	eBay	Chairman	$3.69 billion
David Filo	33	Unfinished PhD Eng at Stanford	Yahoo	Chief Yahoo	$3.12 billion
Jerry Yang	30	Unfinished PhD Eng at Stanford	Yahoo	Chief Yahoo	$3.05 billion
Rob Glaser	37	Former Microsoft VP	Real Networks	Chairman CEO	$2.29 billion
Scott Blum	35	Junior college drop-out	Buy.com		$1.66 billion
Jeff Skoll	33	Another ex-Stanford	eBay	VP	$1.35 billion
Michael Robertson	32		MP3.com	Chairman CEO and president	$903 million
Naveen Jain	39	Ex-Microsoft	InfoSpace.com	Chairman CEO	$861 million
Marc Ewing	30	Ex-IBM	Red Hat	Executive VP, CTO	$775 million
Joe Liemandt	31	Stanford drop-out	Trilogy Software	CEO president	$523 million
Eric Brewer	32	Tenured professor at UCA	Inktomi	Chief scientist	$454 million
Jerry Greenberg	33	Founded the tech consulting firm at 25	Sapient	Co-CEO	$413 million
John Schnatter	37	Pizza!!! Not technology	Papa John's Intl	CEO	$402.6 million
Daniel Snyder	34	College drop-out	Snyder Comms	Chairman CEO	$390 million
Kevin Harvey	35	Backed eBay, Ariba, Red Hat and Scient	Bench-mark Capital Mgmt	Founding partner	$278 million

* As of September 1999

with the new generation. Forget golf weekends for up and coming execs; think bungee jumping. Forget skiing; think snowboarding.

Most people have heard of gen e's big hitters: thirty-somethings like Michael Dell, founder of Dell Corporation, and Jeff Bezos, founder of Amazon.com; and twenty-somethings like the co-founder of Netscape, Marc Andreessen (just 23 when he led a team of programmers that created the web browser Netscape Navigator). Alongside them are a host of others. Their faces have not appeared in *Fast Company* or *Business 2.0* quite so regularly but the youth, entrepreneurial zeal and wealth of people like Dan Snyder of Snyder Communications or Jerry Greenberg of Sapient are equally impressive (Table 1.1).

The list of the young and fabulously wealthy goes on. But this is just the tip of the iceberg – an iceberg that is sinking old-style corporations.

The mass of the iceberg consists of bright sparks in Warsaw, Poland, with smart ideas; software designers in Cork, Ireland; shaven-headed management gurus in Stockholm, Sweden; college drop-outs wired up and wised up sitting in Montana intent on having the lifestyle they want – and think they deserve.

virtual visit   www.webfire.co.uk

The mass of the iceberg is made up of people like computer retailer Tahir Mohsan, founder of Time Computer Systems, who is now worth some £27 million ($44.5 million). Still in his late twenties, Mohsan only set up the company to keep his brother out of trouble. And young aspirants like Gareth Evans who has his own company, Webfire, creating websites. Still a student, he's already talking about employing more people. Gareth is 20 years old. Pure generation e. But his are modest ambitions compared to some. David Koretz thinks big. He aims to be a billionaire, or a multi-millionaire at the very least, by the time he's 25.

Aged 7, Koretz set up shop in his driveway to sell shells. By the age of 10, he had developed a keen interest in the stock market. He started his first real business at 14 – Compucepts, a computer repair service, which evolved into an international electronics distribution firm. He launched the second – a website development business called Webvertisements – when he was a high school senior. In 1997, Koretz shut down Compucepts ('a good educational experience', but never highly profitable) and sold Webvertisements to his partner. This allowed him to concentrate on Network Marketing International (NMI), the business he started when he was 17. In 1998, NMI, a web-based business that generates and distributes sales leads, got financial backing – a healthy injection of venture capital funding. Koretz put his college education on hold. 'Right now, business is pushing the pace of my education a lot faster than I can do at any school,' he says. For some, business is the new education.

Another feature of generation e is the surge of girl power. Once excluded from the entrepreneurial race, a number of the new players are women. Meg Whitman, CEO of eBay, is credited with bringing the discipline and marketing nous that the company needed. Whitman honed her consumer-marketing talents at Hasbro, where she managed the career of Mr Potato Head among other toy stars. Previously she had worked as a marketing executive at Disney. When she was approached by eBay she was comfortably settled on America's East Coast. Her husband, a brain surgeon, was based at Massachusetts General and her kids were in school.

But her entrepreneurial instincts got the better of her. Whitman took a look at the figures and realized the potential. By early 1998 she was leading an eBay team on a roadshow to woo investors. The gamble paid off. On 24 September 1998, the company's IPO (Initial Public Offering) offered eBay shares at a modest $18. By the time the market closed, their value had leapt to $47. Whitman and her eBay colleagues were suddenly rich. Back at the office euphoric staff formed conga lines.

Despite a few glitches – including a series of system crashes in the summer of 1999 which sent eBay stock down 10 per cent – the rewards have been spectacular. eBay has been one of the few dot.coms to generate profits from the word go. In December 1999, the company was valued at more than $20 billion – more than Sears and JC Penny combined. After two years with Whitman at the company's helm, her shares are worth around $1 billion.

United by aspiration, gen e are the new wizards (and their best spells end in

United by aspiration, gen e are the new wizards (and their best spells end in .com). Gen e are driven by business ideas; they are builders of businesses

virtual visit   **www.regus.com**

.com). Gen e are driven by business ideas; they are builders of businesses. Many of them are serial entrepreneurs, with a string of start-ups already under their belts by their early twenties. The entrepreneurial impulse is irresistibly strong.

Mark Dixon, for instance, is a compulsive entrepreneur. The 38-year-old left school at 16 and sold his first sandwich business, Dial-A-Snack, in 1987 for a cool £800,000 ($1.3 million) – not bad for a young man in his twenties. Some people might have retired on the nest egg, but in true entrepreneur fashion he started something else. His new company, called Regus, provides serviced offices to clients, for however long they need them. The company now has a turnover of £130 million ($214.5 million) and is owned lock, stock and barrel by Dixon.

Another of the same ilk is James Lavelle whose life has been lived at such a speed that he should now be approaching middle age. The hyperactive Brit started his own record label Mo' Wax in 1991. Lavelle was 17. The son of a jazz drummer, Lavelle is a fixture in fashionable magazines and has fingers in a variety of musical pies: DJ; remixer; perfomer with his own group U.N.K.L.E.; model. Lavelle has also branched out into the clothing business. He plays down the entrepreneur label, pinning his faith on culture rather than capital – 'I had an original idea which I built up. I was obsessive about it. I've always been an obsessive person.'

From a similar mould is Elwin Giel, the thirty-something Dutch managing director of Power Leisure, the largest leisure group in the Netherlands. His company includes a string of nightclubs, a disco consultancy and an export business for 'electronic cloakrooms'. Giel started his first business at the age of 12 – a mobile disco.

Later, he attended the European Business School in London where he ran a basement disco. He worked for First Leisure in London and as the UK tour manager for Miss World. Giel is the innovator of the 'drinks stockmarket', a concept which he has franchised around the world. Customers are able to influence the price of their drinks through what they buy. They're also allowed to bulk buy and resell their drinks and to take advantage of engineered crashes.

In e world any wacky idea can corner the market. Anything seems possible as an emergent generation seek the biggest and brightest prizes on offer.

from raising hell
to raising capital

The rise of gen e is bad news for traditional corporations – especially for monolithic tie-wearing organizations. People like Gareth Evans or David Koretz are not corporate fodder. Yet, the corporate world depends on a willing army of conscripts. Fresh-faced young recruits keep the wheels turning. But something has changed in the business world. Something significant. The world of big business has lost its allure for many young people – they want to do their own thing. There's a new mood out there. A new spirit. Individual aspirations and ambition are the driving force. Where once faithful employees pursued corporate goals, gen e now dream their own dreams. Gordon Gecko summed up the business culture of the 1980s when he said 'lunch is for wimps'. Gen e believe that 'jobs are for wimps'.

> There's a new mood out there. A new spirit. Individual aspirations and ambition are the driving force

A dramatic change can be seen at the world's leading business schools. For the average MBA, the career plan used to be to step from the b-school comfort zone and suckle the corporate bosom. Most wanted nothing better than to work for one of the big name investment banks or consulting firms. No longer. A growing proportion of b-school graduates are shunning a job with a blue chip company in favour of something more racy, something nearer the entrepreneurial edge.

Nearly one-third of MBA graduates from Harvard Business School joined high tech or venture capital companies in 1998. In 1995 the figure was a mere 12 per cent.[5] Viva e! 'Today, 20 per cent of Harvard MBAs join companies with fewer than 100 people, and 20 per cent of Stanford MBAs join companies with fewer than 50.

Yeah, some still want to go into consulting and devote their lives

virtual visit   www.hbs.edu

to making the world safe for vice presidents, but more and more want to go kick incumbent butt.' So says Gary Hamel, visiting professor at London Business School and one of the world's acknowledged strategy gurus.[6] Incumbents beware.

Increasingly, too, the business plans of MBA students are picked up by venture capitalists. This is a match made in entrepreneurial heaven. The business plan competitions run by the top b-schools have become rich hunting grounds. They have become an industry in themselves – MIT's Entrepreneurship Competition has a $50,000 prize. Zefer, an internet consulting firm, won the business plan competition at Harvard Business School in 1998 and went on to attract funding of $100 million. It now has over 400 employees, attracts big name execs and has offices throughout the USA. Akami, a loser in MIT's competition, brought in $43 million. The 1998 winner of the MIT competition, Direct Hit, was so flush with cash that it returned the prize money. (This is the first recorded instance of students of any sort turning down a cash handout.) Not surprisingly, among the MBA business plans, internet start-ups are highly fashionable – accounting for 38 out of 68 teams entering Stanford's 1999 competition.

Everywhere is Hollywood. Bright young things no longer have a movie script in their back pocket but a .com business plan. And entrepreneurs are getting

younger all the time. For many young people, business has

virtual visit   www.zefer.com

become the new rock and roll. They still hang out in their parents' garage, but it's not songs they're writing; it's software – and a business plan. Now they dream of .com start-ups. Where once they aspired to be the next Kurt Cobain, now they invent a different nirvana – an IPO that can make them richer than God. Forget raising hell; raise capital instead. Who wants to be the next Liam Gallagher, when you could be the next Jeff Bezos? Whose picture was on the cover of *Time* magazine's last issue of the century? None other than Jeff Preston Bezos. The magazine's 'person of the year' for 1999, Bezos is the fourth-youngest individual honoured in this way, preceded only by 25-year-old Charles Lindbergh in 1927; Queen Elizabeth II, who made the list in 1952 at the age of 26; and Martin Luther King Jr, who was 34 when he was selected in 1963. A pioneer, royalty and a revolutionary seem appropriate company for the Amazon man.

> Everywhere is Hollywood. Bright young things no longer have a movie script in their back pocket but a .com business plan

Bezos is one of the legends of gen e. In his mid-thirties, the Amazon.com founder is already an icon. His wealth, accumulated in the space of just four years, is estimated at between $5 and depending on Amazon's share price $10.5 billion. Such is the speed with which his life moves that the crown prince of the net (Bezos will ascend to the throne the day Amazon announces profits) is concerned that he won't remember

www.amazon.com **virtual visit**

the details. He carries a camera around with him to capture the moment. Perhaps it is simply to reassure him that it is really happening. His rise has been so meteoric – his story so incredible – that he feels the need for documentary proof. (Another who should be making movies is Michael Dell, perhaps the greatest of all the new entrepreneurs and now worth more than $20 billion – and he's a decade younger than Bill Gates.)

Future documentaries will confirm that since the mid-1990s, Bezos and other gen e stars have been busy revolutionizing the business world. Companies that have been around just a few

> Gen e are making the sort of money that corporate man could only dream of

years like Amazon.com and eBay are valued more highly than long-established rivals. Take a snapshot. On 1 June 1999, for example, the market capitalization of Sears, Roebuck was $19.2 billion. United Airlines had a market cap of $4.1 billion and auction house Sotheby's was capitalized at a lowly $1.7 billion. Contrast them with some upstarts – eBay with a market cap of $22.1 billion, Priceline.com at $18.6 billion, and Amazon.com with a market capitalization of $22 billion.[7] Gen e are making the sort of money that corporate man could only dream of.

This is already having a major impact on big business. Unthinkable just a few

> The Fortune 500 is now the Misfortune 500. It's more than just a changing of the old guard: it's a palace coup on a grand scale

virtual visit   **www.mbs.ac.uk**

> Corporate man is dead. Long live generation entrepreneur!

years ago, the Fortune 500 – a mere 9 per cent of the US economy – is no longer where it's at. The Fortune 500 is now the Misfortune 500. It's more than just a changing of the old guard: it's a palace coup on a grand scale. Companies and business schools are trying to get in on the act. The UK's Manchester Business School recently launched a new executive programme in spring 2000 simply called e – with e standing for experience, e-business and (immodestly) exceptional leadership. Today, everyone is a potential Michael Dell or Larry Ellison. The battle for the new technologically based wealth is the gold rush of the late twentieth century. But it's just the start. The twenty-first century heralds bigger changes. Corporate man is dead. Long live generation entrepreneur!

Chapter 3

The bagel queen

Gen e travel some previously obscure paths. How about this route: from investment banking to bagel baking. In 1997 Danielle Downing gave up a well-paid job with Salomon Brothers to start Bagel Street, a bagel deli chain, in London. Born in NYC (where else would a bagel entrepreneur be from?), Downing took an MBA at Wharton and, after graduating in 1992, headed east – to Russia to be precise, where she spent the next five years.

> From investment banking to bagel baking

'At the time it was the wild west capitalism in Russia. I went originally with the intention of setting up the bagel business there.' But the reality, when she arrived, didn't inspire her with confidence. 'Everything took such a long time. I got really frustrated. Just negotiating a lease was problematic, and even if you found the right premises you knew someone might show up with an Uzi one day and say that the place belonged to him now.'

She put her own plans on the back burner for a while. With western banks only too keen to recruit people who knew their way around, she joined Salomon Brothers as an equity strategist and stayed for two years. The job was challenging and lucrative, but something was missing.

'There was no incentive programme to encourage you to work as a team at

Salomon Brothers. Rewards were linked to individual performance. I think that's what pushed me out in the end.' Like other entrepreneurs, Downing says, there was an element of push and an element of pull that created the spark for action. 'The logical plank is that you convince yourself that the numbers make sense. But the push is that you believe you can do more than what you're doing.'

'I was never really a banker. I was an entrepreneur working for a bank,' explains the 35-year-old. 'I remember I was in some boring meeting in Portugal, and I just thought this isn't what I want to do with my life.'

> Time to dust off the bagel deli business plan. Her research showed that the average American ate 30 bagels a year, while average bagel consumption in the UK was about two

Time to dust off the bagel deli business plan. Her research showed that the average American ate 30 bagels a year, while average bagel consumption in the UK was about two. There were other indications that the UK market was ready for a bagel invasion. In the US, the spread of bagel stores had coincided with an increase in awareness and their arrival in supermarkets – prompted by Kellogg's and other big chains buying up bagel brands. In Europe, Kraft had just acquired a major bagel wholesaler. London beckoned.

The success of Starbucks in the UK also suggested the British were ready for American-style stores – and provided a useful template for a revamped business plan. 'It's not like I'm reinventing the wheel here,' says Downing. 'I'm taking best practice from others and applying it to a different market.' 'The fact that it had been tried and had already succeeded in the US was part of the story. I talked to a lot of people who believed in the idea. I'm a business person: I tapped into my business network. Friends in investment banking and friends of friends. I raised about £1 million ($1.65 million) that way.'

> Next stop was bagel school

Next stop was bagel school. 'We learned about yeast and flour and all that stuff, but my aim was to network among the bagel community. I wanted to recruit a master bagel maker. I'm not a baker. You'd never want to eat the bagel I made,' she says with admirable frankness. 'But I know enough about bagels to know how I want them to taste.'

She then had to persuade UK immigration to give her new recruit the necessary work visa. 'I had to convince them that there really wasn't anyone over here who could do the job – that there weren't any master bagel bakers in the UK.' But Downing knew that simply transplanting the American formula into the UK wasn't the way to go. In the US, she knew, New Yorkers and Californians have distinctive tastes in bagel texture. Local adaptation was clearly in order.

'If I sold American bagels here British people wouldn't want them,' she observes. Testing with customers indicated that a distinctive British bagel recipe was required. (A more bready product, she says, so that it lends itself to sandwiches.) Size was also an issue. The British don't like to throw away food, so Bagel Street offers a 'mini bagel' as well as the traditional NY monster.

The first Bagel Street store opened in September 1999 in Hampstead, London. 'Hampstead has a strong Jewish community, lots of bankers who have spent some time working on Wall Street, and an American community, too,' Downing explains. The Hampstead store is family oriented, with cartoons featuring bagels – what else? – for children to colour in.

The second store opened in December 1999 and has a very different personality. Located in the City, opposite the Old Bailey, it is aimed at the business community. A 24-hour store in Soho is scheduled to open in spring 2000 and will be targeted at young people out for a night's clubbing. Downing's ambitious plan is to have a chain of 50 stores in the UK in the next few years. Long live the bagel queen and her loyal regime.

e isn't x

Crude attempts have been made to capture gen e in a neat demographical box. Try to package our bagel queen as a sociological or demographical grouping and you end up with a group of one. Celebration is more appropriate than categorization.

That doesn't stop people trying. Gen e have been defined, for example, as those born between 1965 and 1977.[8] This overlaps with Generation X, named after Douglas Coupland's 1991 novel. Generation X was always a loose term to describe a fragmented group. Gen Xers were portrayed as shiftless and unambitious people. The lost generation, slackers. More apathetic than previous generations, nihilistic even, the stereotypical Gen Xer was addicted to MTV, lacked drive or a basic work ethic and drifted from one McJob to the next. This made a good story and fitted in with the nihilistic and short-lived grunge movement in music.

> More apathetic than previous generations, nihilistic even, the stereotypical Gen Xer was addicted to MTV, lacked drive or a basic work ethic and drifted from one McJob to the next

However, it was only partly true. One good album does not make for lasting impact. The reality is that Generation X was never a homogeneous group. It was a neat label for social change. Demographically speaking, gen e is largely a subset of Gen X, which now extends to Generation Y (born between 1979 and

1994 – in the US alone this amounts to some 60 million people; three times as many as there are in Gen X).[9]

We are not much interested in demographics and nor are venture capitalists: a good business idea is a good business idea; a smart entrepreneur is a smart entrepreneur regardless of their age, social status, or shoe size. In reality, gen e is much more about new patterns of thinking than it is a hard and fast demographic grouping. Typically in their late twenties to mid-thirties, gen e are not distinguished by their date of birth, but by their attitude. Gen e is inclusive. There are 50-year-olds with gen e attitude, just as there are 20-year-old dinosaurs.

> In reality, gen e is much more about new patterns of thinking than it is a hard and fast demographic grouping

Clearly there are overlaps between different generational groupings. But people are not lumpen masses, easily contained or constrained by demographic or any other pigeonholing. Bruce Tulgan wrote the influential book *Managing Generation X*. In it he tried to distil the work ethic of his generation. Tulgan himself is pure gen e; he left Wall Street in 1994 to start Rainmaker Thinking, a firm which researches the working lives of Gen Xers. Some, though not all, of his conclusions ring true for gen e. In *Work This Way*, he describes the 'post jobs era'.[10] 'It's all over,' he says. 'All of it. Not just job security. Jobs are all over. We have entered the post jobs era and there's no turning back.'

Jay A. Conger, a former visiting professor at Harvard Business School and INSEAD, and now based at the University of Southern California, has carried out extensive interviews with Generation X managers, and confirms a significant shift in attitudes. 'In a nutshell they distrust hierarchy,' he says. 'They prefer more informal arrangements. They prefer to judge – and be judged – on merit rather than on status. They are also far less loyal to their companies.' Again, we believe this is generally true of gen e.

> e stands for entrepreneurial, but it's also for energy – and much more

While the overlaps between e and X are many and varied, differences also abound. They are divided by more than the rest of the alphabet. Gen X were portrayed as apathetic; but gen e are prepared to work long hours to get a business off the ground. They are driven – sometimes obsessively. e stands for entrepreneurial, but it's also for energy – and much more. Gen e are an increasingly powerful group in the business world. Many are in the vanguard of the new economy, either running their own businesses or occupying management positions within established companies. But their attitudes towards employers mean the way they approach their careers is very different from that of their predecessors. To understand the way they think, you have to understand the events which shaped them.

They are better educated than their predecessors. They share the Baby Boomers' dislike of hierarchy: they are more freewheeling group than carefully delineated pyramid. Most of all, they are shamelessly entrepreneurial. A few start out with grand visions in mind. But most just don't want to work in traditional corporate hierarchies. They're willing to borrow money from friends and relatives and even run their credit cards up to the hilt to get a business off the ground. Ted Waitt, the 36-year-old founder of Gateway, started the company with a $10,000 loan guaranteed by his grandmother. Just over a decade later, Gateway has revenues in excess of $6 billion.

www.gateway.com | virtual visit

When Jeff Bezos quit his job to set up Amazon, his mother and stepfather invested $300,000 saved for their retirement in the venture, even though they had no idea what the internet was. Everyone starts somewhere. The vital difference between Generation X and gen e is that the latter are more likely to know where they are going. They are certainly clear about where they are not going. A dull corporate existence is not an option.

> The vital difference between Generation X and gen e is that the latter are more likely to know where they are going. They are certainly clear about where they are not going. A dull corporate existence is not an option

dollars and amazonians

Consider this. On the morning of 28 September 1999, Jeff Bezos of Amazon.com let it be known that on the following morning he would be making an announcement about the future direction of his business. It was, he said, 'an announcement significantly affecting the world of e-commerce'. Such pronouncements are not unusual. CEOs routinely claim their businesses are making earth-shattering moves in their markets. Usually, they aren't. But when Bezos talks, the business world listens.

The American business press dropped everything to rush to the hotel where Bezos was speaking. It is not uncommon for the stock of a company to rise or fall when news is imminent. But on this occasion in Silicon Valley and on Wall Street there was a frenzy of speculation. By the end of the day, with no news other than the announcement of the announcement, the market valuation of Amazon.com had jumped by $1.5 billion.[11] This, remember, was before Bezos even opened his mouth.

Gen e increasingly set the agenda. They are now the movers and shakers of the business world. When Jeff Bezos announces he intends to talk, people get ready to listen. Venerated as the John Doe (Joe Bloggs) of e-commerce, Bezos has become the ultimate gen e icon. If Bill Gates is the archetypal nerd, Bezos is the ordinary guy who proves that e-commerce is the business goldmine.

Back in 1994, Bezos, a Princeton graduate in computer science and electrical engineering, was a young senior vice-president at a thriving Wall Street hedge fund. (D.E. Shaw, where Bezos worked, is an unusual firm that prides itself on hiring some of the smartest people in the world, and then finding something profitable for them to do with their time. Bezos was 'sort of an entrepreneurial odd-jobs kind of person', the company's founder David Shaw recently recalled.[12] His job was to think up business opportunities.) That's when the explosive growth of the World Wide Web grabbed his attention. Surfing the net one day Bezos came upon a fascinating statistic – Web usage was growing at a rate of 2,300 per cent a month. (This may or may not have been true. Bezos certainly acted as if he believed it.) Online commerce, he realized, was a natural next step. Part Wall Street insider and part computer nerd, Bezos was perfectly placed to cash in.

> Venerated as the John Doe of e-commerce, Bezos has become the ultimate gen e icon

Bezos drew up a shortlist of 20 products he thought could be successfully sold over the Web. The list included music, magazines, computer software and hardware – and books. The list was shortened to books and music. In the end books won for two simple reasons. First, he reasoned that with more than 1.3 million books in print versus 300,000 music titles, there were more to sell.

Second, and perhaps more importantly, the big publishers seemed less intimidating. They didn't appear to have the same sort of stranglehold on the business as the six major record companies that dominate music. The biggest book chain, Barnes and Noble, accounted for less than 12 per cent of the industry's $25 billion in annual sales.

'There are no 800-pound gorillas in book publishing or distribution,' Bezos observed. The decision made, Bezos quit his job and packed his bags. Then folklore kicks in. Bezos's wife, the improbably named MacKenzie, drove them cross-country in a Chevy Blazer, while Bezos sat in the passenger seat pounding out a business plan on a laptop computer and negotiating seed capital on his mobile phone. 'I will change the economics of the book industry as a whole,' he is reputed to have told one venture capitalist with quotable bravura. Ironically, fund raising was also carried out in the coffee shop of his local Barnes and Noble bookstore.

Bezos knew he needed to base his operation in a state without a state tax, and settled on the Seattle area because of the richness of high-tech talent and the presence of a major book distributor – Ingram's warehouse – down the road in Roseberg, Oregon. In classic high-tech-start-up style, Bezos and his first three employees set up computers in the garage of their rented home in the Seattle suburb of Bellevue. They were already busy writing the software that would support the new business model before the furniture even caught up with them. The rest, you might think, is history. Not quite.

Bezos originally decided to call his new company Cadabra, with the magical incantation in mind. But friends talked him out of it, explaining that it sounded a bit like cadaver. Reasoning that it would carry many more books than conventional stores, he opted for Amazon, after the world's largest river.

Launched as a website in July 1995, by the beginning of 1999 Amazon.com Inc. had a market capitalization of $6 billion – more than the combined value of Barnes and Noble and Borders, its two biggest bookstore competitors online and off. In the fourth quarter of 1998, net sales were $252.9 million, an increase of 283 per cent over the same period in 1997.

> Bezos is the exemplar of the e-myth, the entrepreneur with an idea who made good. The fact that his company has yet to make a cent in profit tends to be forgotten along the way. Why spoil the story?

Bezos is the exemplar of the e-myth, the entrepreneur with an idea who made good. The fact that his company has yet to make a cent in profit tends to be forgotten along the way.[13] Why spoil the story? (For the record, Bezos has now said that Amazon's book, music and video product lines will all be profitable by the end of 2000 – an event called 'BMVP 2000' in Amazon parlance.)

defining a generation

a little bit hyperkinetic

D efining what an entrepreneur does is relatively straightforward. 'A person who undertakes an enterprise or business, with the chance of profit or loss,' says the dictionary.[14] But pinpointing what makes someone an entrepreneur is problematic. The characteristics of entrepreneurs have been debated for centuries. As with leadership, with which entrepreneurship is closely linked, it is hard to put your finger on what makes a successful entrepreneur.

Tim Waterstone, founder of the eponymous book chain and successful entrepreneur, observes some common traits. Great entrepreneurs, he notes, share the following characteristics. They:

- Are inspirational leaders
- Believe their vision is right and don't falter in their belief
- Derive energy from being the underdog
- Are driven by a strong desire to beat the competition – to defeat the enemy
- Combine enormous energy with fortitude and tenacity
- Demonstrate courage – by taking risks

- Have a deep respect for the people in their team and value team building
- Understand how money works. Not necessarily in a technical way, but in an intuitive way.

Many of these ring true to gen e, but gen e has its own distinctive characteristics. So, what are the characteristics of gen e? What general traits do they possess? First, e = energy. Gen e are dynamic, restless creators. What makes them tick? Wrong question. Gen e people don't tick, they buzz. 'I always run through the office,' says Jeff Bezos. 'I mean physically I'm a little bit hyperkinetic. That's why I like this environment.' If you see a man with a camera running towards you it could well be Bezos.

e = energy

Gen e people don't tick, they buzz

High energy levels are vital for entrepreneurial success. There aren't many lazy success stories out there. Energy is a prerequisite for the job. 'One of the things I look for most in people is energy levels,' says Robert Devereux, CEO of Virgin Group. 'I won't employ people who don't have high energy levels, because they won't last. Because people with energy, they're self-motivated, they get going, they get things done.'[15]

Energy drives and changes businesses both old and new. Gen e don't just ignite new businesses, they re-ignite those which have stagnated.

Gen e don't just ignite new businesses, they re-ignite those which have stagnated

Liisa Joronen runs a Finnish cleaning and waste management company, SOL. She has turned a dull and dirty business into something special. In 1992 Joronen's father split up the family business, a national laundry chain called Lindstrom. Joronen took over the company's cleaning operations. 'There I was on 1 January 1992 with 2,200 people and 2,500 customers not knowing quite what to do. The economic situation in Finland was really bad. Fortunately, some of the best people at Lindstrom took a personal risk and followed me. We moved very quickly, changed the name to SOL and adopted a completely new identity based on the philosophy that employees must be given the chance to perform at their best.'

Joronen challenged conventional culture. She sloganized ('Kill routine before it kills you', 'Freedom from the office') abandoned traditional Finnish working hours and introduced teamworking. Worker participation is now integral to the way the company operates. Staff were asked to help design the first SOL headquarters – SOL Studio – in a converted film studio in Helsinki. More than 1,200 concepts for the ideal workplace were generated through a series of workshops. The ideas were then developed in dialogue with management and a team of interior designers and were implemented in a record-breaking five weeks. (The process was repeated when the company moved to its current larger premises – SOL City.)

> Joronen has injected fun, energy and enthusiasm into a moribund business

The new way of working means that the time staff spend in the office is entirely up to them. They are judged purely on results. The company has also dispensed with the conventional trappings of authority: supervisors are 'peer counsellors', desks are communal and no one has a secretary.

SOL weathered the recession and now has a turnover of $50 million and is growing at an annual rate of 20 to 25 per cent. Joronen has injected fun, energy and enthusiasm into a moribund business.[16]

> For gen e, how they spend their time, how they enthuse others is more important than the hours they work. Quality is vital; quantity is no longer a competitive advantage

There is a difference between possessing energy and being a seriously hard worker. Maximizing entrepreneurial energy is more than running fast or working harder. Anyone can work 16 hours a day. For gen e, how they spend their time, how they enthuse others is more important than the hours they work. Quality is vital; quantity is no longer a competitive advantage. Quantity is never quality.

The energy characteristic of gen e leads them to question what others assume. Gen e liberate energy in others. Their belief and desire to change things give them energy and inspire others. They discover energy from the mundane, from the routine. They extract ideas to generate enthusiasm. They invent different approaches and try new things. They generate energy from themselves and stimulate energy out of those they work with. They attract people with energy.

united distillers

T he second characteristic of gen e is an ability to focus energy and thinking on the issues, trends and people that really matter; e = essence. Energy is channelled to the essence of what is important.

$e = essence$

The ability to cut out the dross, the distracting stuff, has never been more important. Choice and complexity can overwhelm. The supply of information and opinions leaders receive is incredibly complex. Every hour 100 million telephone calls are made using 300 million lines across the world. Despite the flood of calls, letters, faxes and e-mails, gen e make sense of it and extract the important details from the vast bulk of paper and input from a wide variety of sources. No matter what, they keep communication as simple as possible. They distil information and insights as keenly as the Jack Daniels team distil spirit at Lynchburg, Tennessee.

Simplification is a necessary evil. If you are to sell an idea in a complex environment it has to convince people – and quick. To be petite is to be perfectly formed. 'Say you have a meeting and someone goes home at night and the next day there's a ten-page memo that's crisp in evaluating the ideas – that's a smart piece of work. In software, it's not like ditch-digging where the best is two or three times faster than the average. The best software writer is the one who can make the program small, make it clever,' says Bill Gates.[17] At one company executives giving presentations are restricted to no more than three overheads.

There are so many bright ideas out there that venture capitalists want killer business plans delivered on the back of a microchip. The trend is for pithy business plans. David Ishag of the internet investment firm Idealab says: 'Plans have to be light as a feather. You have to be able to make your case in an elevator – and I'm talking about an elevator in a very low building.'[18]

Gen e are adept at crystallizing ideas. It is always easy to make things complicated; far harder to make things simple. 'Simplicity means figuring out how to hide complexity. That takes a lot of code,' said Compaq marketing director Dave Hocker back in 1993.[19] In the 1980s, BA's Nick Georgiades poignantly described the work of cabin crew as 'emotional labour'. Similarly, Disney's Michael Eisner came up with the phrase 'high concept' to describe a brilliant idea which can be condensed into a single persuasive sentence. (The writer of the screenplay *Twins* reputedly condensed the film into six words – 'Arnold Schwarzenegger, Danny de Vito, twins' – to persuade studio moguls to back it: they did.) Gen e continually develop their own high concepts.

> There are so many bright ideas out there that venture capitalists want killer business plans delivered on the back of a microchip. The trend is for pithy business plans

Distilling messages inspires. It renders hazy generics lifting. When the US invaded Panama in 1989 the operation was given the code name 'Blue Spoon'. Colin Powell changed it to 'Just Cause' – 'You do not risk people's lives for blue spoons,' he explained.[20] Similarly, gen e distil to motivate – themselves and others.

Staff at Amazon.com are encouraged to join a crusade. Nine-to-fivers need not apply. The company sees its mission as changing both how people shop and how they think about shopping. 'It's like the Cultural Revolution meets Sam Walton. It's dotcommunism!' one journalist wrote of the Amazon culture after spending a day with Bezos.[21] Employees are offered the opportunity not just to make money, but to make history, by making the cyberstore a success. 'Our vision is the world's most customer-centric company,' says an Amazon banner.

'The place where people come to find and discover anything they might want to buy online.'

At times this can appear the business equivalent of the sound bite, the business bite. Business bites distil complex issues into punchy one-liners. Forget the detailed academic argument. The idea is to capture the very essence of your business philosophy or message into a simple but highly memorable sentence. 'IBM was yesterday; Microsoft is today; Oracle is the future,' says Larry Ellison with customary elan. In so doing, the owner and originator hopes to achieve two not entirely unrelated objectives. First, to become instantly recognizable to managers around the globe; and second, to sell business books and consultancy services.

The intellectual sound bites are phrases such as *Only the Paranoid Survive,* a bestseller for Andrew Grove, head of Intel. We can only guess at how the book might have fared had his original altogether less snappy title *Navigating Strategic Inflection Points* not been rejected by the publisher.

'A PC in every home' could only be Bill Gates. If anything, the bites are getting noticeably more audacious. eBay's 'eBay everywhere', for example, proclaims omnipresence. Business bites differ sharply from mission statements – which are typically bland corporate statements. They typically belong to the individual rather than the company. So, for example, 'Any color you like as long as it's black' goes with Henry Ford and not with the eponymous car company he founded.

Some have been quicker on the uptake than others. The man who coined the phrase 'nanosecond nineties', Tom Peters, has had more bites than just about anyone. More recently, his bite has been: 'Crazy times call for crazy organizations'.

Business bites are important business weapons. No business leaders ever achieved anything if they weren't understood. At their best, they communicate complex ideas simply, quickly and understandably. At worst, they are meaningless bastardizations.

Such is the premium placed on business bites that it is not unheard of for them to be followed by the copyright symbol © or even the letters ™ denoting trade-marks of the author. This is more likely where there are consultancy products and services to be sold on the back of the intellectual property they represent. Messages must bite.

only connect

The third ingredient in the make-up of gen e is that they are wired; e = electronic. No surprise. When it comes to new technology they get it in a way most big companies can

e = electronic

only dream of. 'The nerds have won,' management guru Tom Peters proclaimed when the market valuation of Microsoft exceeded that of General Motors. Nerds – geeks – techies – we've invented labels for them, but the reality is that, increasingly, they are the people who call the tune.

Nerds – geeks – techies – we've invented labels for them, but the reality is that, increasingly, they are the people who call the tune

Again the crucial difference is one of focus and perception. Gen e regard technology as crucial in a number of key areas.

First, technology allows for cost-effective organization. Forget about all that mortar, all those bricks. Gen e are as comfortable working from their bedroom as from a tower block. Second, it facilitates constant communication. To distil things down, you have to talk a lot in the first place. Third, it enables flexible working. Technology switches work on, whenever, wherever. And, fourth, it gives you a direct route to customers. Most importantly of all, technology delivers you to the living room of the consumer every moment of every day.

If you can bring all of these elements together then you are really harnessing

37

technology. It is surprising how few companies have managed to do so. But some pull it off. Among those who have done so is Richard Nissen. 'At the beginning of the 1990s everyone was talking about using technology to work virtually. I thought it was going to happen,' he says. Unlike most people, Richard Nissen set out to turn virtual working into reality. After leaving his family's company, he set up a serviced office business in Piccadilly. This grew quickly and in 1989 moved to 211 Piccadilly – just 50 yards from Piccadilly Circus. Then, in 1994, Nissen created the first telephone call handling platform that could fully support flexible working practices, with calls being patched through to individuals wherever they were. The Virtual Office was underway.

Now, the Virtual Office has over 1,200 clients, sales of £2 million and four buildings in London, as well as connections with business centres elsewhere in the UK, in South Korea and worldwide through the Global Office Network.

The Virtual Office creates a virtual circle. Technology means that calls can be connected instantly, no matter where the recipient is located. Though a central London number is called, the Virtual Office client can be standing in the middle of a Welsh field with a mobile phone. At the same time, companies can benefit from having virtual secretaries who can organize such things as travel itineraries and accommodation. A prestigious city centre address is part of the allure. Then there is the networking through the Virtual Office Club. The Virtual Office's clients are usually smaller companies keen to maximize and focus their resources.

'Managers haven't changed enough. They remain addicted to treating people as if they were at school instead of telling them to go away and do something as they would do at university. The office is a construct of the late nineteenth century'

While the Virtual Office thrives, Richard Nissen is the first to admit that virtual working has not taken off to the extent he and others anticipated. First, he attributes this to managerial attitudes. 'Old style managers hate not seeing their people. They want to see people working at their desks,' he says. 'Managers haven't changed enough. They remain addicted to treating people as if they were at school instead of telling them to go away and do something as they would do at university. The office is a construct of the late nineteenth century.' The second obstacle has been that virtual working is often seen as a technical issue. Responsibility is therefore passed to the IT department, which would rather computing equipment stayed in the building.

The third factor is that of costs. Richard Nissen argues that companies often have very little idea about the overheads attached to the people they employ. While companies rigorously analyze costs in a host of other areas, the price of having someone sitting at a desk is usually overlooked. This, predicts Nissen, will have to change. 'In the early 1990s companies tended to have spare space after reducing managerial numbers. Now they tend not to and are more inclined to calculate how much space costs in terms of per head per annum. Usually this works out to around £10,000 a year. Once this figure is established, there is a driver for change.'

This contention that companies have little idea as to these crucial costs is backed up by work by the management consulting firm Booz-Allen and Hamilton into what it calls 'non-product related expenditures'. It estimates that companies typically spend around 20 to 25 per cent of sales with third-party suppliers for goods and services which are not directly related to the end product of their business. These costs include such things as office supplies, security, mail handling and travel. Among the most significant of these costs are those for building services, real estate and property management. Booz-Allen and Hamilton estimates that examination of these costs can reap significant savings – for example, typically 5 to 10 per cent can be knocked off property management costs.

www.bah.com | virtual visit

Given such potential savings, it is little wonder that Richard Nissen believes the next frontier for virtual working lies in bringing the concept to the wider corporate world. 'Companies with good IT infrastructures are beginning to contemplate different ways of costing their people,' he says. 'This may involve putting people in business centres. We have the software to enable companies to actually bill people for the corporate resources they use. People could receive an itemized bill for using meeting rooms for example.'

There is, Richard Nissen admits, a hint of Big Brother about the potential uses to which information can now be put in the workplace. 'There is a degree of paranoia in the working environment. As we are able to gather more data, this is perhaps inevitable. The motivation must be to use the data now available to give people the freedom to work as they want.' The dividing line between freedom and control is a thin one. Virtual freedom may come, but it will almost certainly have a price attached.

trained to the max

G en e trait no. 4: e = educated. More than ever before, education equals money. (It also equals efficiency: a 1995 study by the National Center of the Educational Quality of the

e = educated

Workforce looked at 3,100 US workplaces. The research found that an average 10 per cent increase in the workforce's educational level led to an 8.6 per cent increase in productivity. In contrast, a 10 per cent increase in plant and equipment increased productivity by 3.4 per cent.) Thomas Stewart of *Fortune* reports that the only group of American men to make gains in their real weekly earnings since 1979 are college graduates, who are now paid an average of 80 per cent more than high school graduates. In the new economy, it pays to have an education. Where once entrepreneurs pooh-poohed a formal business education, gen e are trained to the max. 'There was a time when all the smart MBAs went into consulting and investment banking,' notes Harvard's William Sahlman. 'Now they're becoming entrepreneurs or zipping off to Silicon Valley to join an existing team, where they can turn the cranks and pull the levers that make the new economy thrive.'

In response to demand, the entrepreneurial spirit has returned to the world's business schools. More than one-third of INSEAD MBAs end up running their own

41

company five to ten years after graduating. Among INSEAD's entrepreneurial alumni is Paul Chantler, managing director of the Paris Real Ale Brewery. Chantler's inspiration came through INSEAD's new ventures elective. This led to a business plan for a micro-brewery and the creation, with a fellow MBA graduate, of an English-style pub and micro-brewery in Paris.

virtual visit **www.insead.fr**

Among those taking the new ventures elective when we visited INSEAD in fall 1999 was Adam Norwitt. He is dissecting the potential of an internet-related start-up in a group made up of himself, an American, an Irishman and a Mexican. It is, he says, a melting pot of ideas and potential. 'We each bring knowledge that's very useful. The Mexican guy knows the internet. The Irishman is a former software engineer. You might not be able to bring such a group together anywhere else,' says the former lawyer.

Other schools point to their track records with enthusiasm. Spain's Instituto de Empresa in Madrid strongly emphasizes entrepreneurialism. The subject is part of the compulsory MBA curriculum and also offered as an elective. In the last ten years, more than 350 companies have been set up by Instituto students – each employing an average of ten employees. The school calculates that this amounts to £2.25 billion worth of investment.

virtual visit **www.ie.edu**

The UK's Cranfield School of Management points to the success of Robert Wright, a 1982 graduate, as an example of what can be done. Wright took the entrepreneurship and planning your own business electives on Cranfield's MBA programme and went on to launch his own airline, eventually sold for £6.25 million. His current venture is CityFlyer Express which has a turnover of over £89 million.

Given such figures it is little wonder that business schools and their students are anxious to board the entrepreneurial bandwagon. London Business School MBA students have formed an E-Club to co-ordinate and promote entrepreneurship within the School. The club has over 200 members and is indicative of a change in emphasis at the School since John

virtual visit **www.lbs.ac.uk**

Quelch took over as dean. Professor Quelch has identified entrepreneurship as one of the School's main priorities. It has £4 million available to fund student start-ups through a venture capital fund.

The entrepreneurial trend means that schools are sometimes to be found taking the leap themselves. Cambridge University's Judge Institute of Management Studies has recently announced plans for the Cambridge Entrepreneurship Centre. Most notably, **www.jims.cam.ac.uk** virtual visit Imperial College has established a number of spin-off companies and estimates that around 750 people are now employed in 37 companies which originated from technologies developed at the College. Imperial's MBA programme includes a 120-hour specialization in entrepreneurship and innovation. This is run by Professor Sue Birley who regards the entrepreneurial spirit **www.ms.ic.ac.uk** virtual visit as being intrinsic to Imperial's role. 'I believe the creation and sharing of intellectual property to be the core role of a university – its prime asset. Managing it for commercial profit is a serious future challenge,' she says.

One problem facing schools is that the world is hardly awash with academics with specialist entrepreneurial knowledge. 'There is new emphasis on entrepreneurship though there is shortage of faculty in that area,' admits INSEAD dean Antonio Borges. 'We are responding to a perceived need for the future. The fast-growing, very innovative, high-risk companies pose questions as to how they should best be managed. We must help answer those questions as those companies will be one of the main drivers of the world of management in ten years' time.'

While all this is true, you may raise an eyebrow after a series of European examples. What about US b-schools? Aren't Stanford and the like way ahead when it comes to entrepreneurialism? Perhaps they are, but don't assume it to be the case. As we will see, gen e is global, truly global. MBA students in Madrid are as entrepreneurial as those at Stanford in the midst of Silicon Valley. Believe otherwise and you are playing a dangerous game.

the calling

Gen e trait no. 5: e = enthusiasm. To top off energy, gen e are natural enthusiasts. For gen e the job itself provides a reservoir of energy. The job matters. (They are not the only ones: why else is Jack Welch running GE after a triple bypass, and why is Michael Eisner at Disney after his heart attack? Why is Rupert Murdoch still putting deals together?)

e = enthusiasm

For gen e, business is a vocation – a calling. They want to work with other highly motivated people. A 21-year-old Cambridge student described herself as 'not ambitious, not competitive, but intensely motivated'. Gen e are passionate about work. They blur the divide between business and private lives. They bring their emotions to work along with their laptops.

'Some people think enthusiasm at work is childish. We reject that notion. Emotion, enthusiasm, energy, passion, whatever you call it, is the lifeblood of entrepreneurial activity,' write Matt Kingdon, Dave Allan, Kris Murrin and Daz Rudkin, the founders of the innovation consultancy ?What If!. 'Too many managers have erected barriers to protect themselves from these very emotions. We believe that in time, creative revolutionaries will swarm over this barricade. They will demand to know why emotions are excluded from a large proportion of people's lives. They will throw off the chains traditional managers have shackled themselves and others with. Yes, we are passionate about this.'

A major US auto manufacturer carries out training in enthusiasm. Wonderful idea. Enthusiasm should be carefully cultivated and nurtured. After all, it is highly infectious. Go to a Tom Peters seminar and, even if you do not remember a single idea, you will remember that Peters is an enthusiast who can transmit his enthusiasm so that people begin to believe in their own potential. Gen e transmit enthusiasm.

Paradoxically, energy and enthusiasm are not hard work. Really effective energy doesn't look as if it is energy at all. It looks energy-less. Great energy slows time – look at great athletes. They appear to have all the time in the world.

> Paradoxically, energy and enthusiasm are not hard work. Really effective energy doesn't look as if it is energy at all

Esa-Pekka Salonen, principal conductor with the Los Angeles Philharmonic, says: 'The main thing is to motivate – to try to release the energies and passion in different individuals in order to make them feel free, to create the illusion that they are actually doing what they are doing and not being led by somebody. That is when the best results happen. In the best possible case, the illusion of freedom becomes true. They are free.'[22] Gen e set people free.

Only the enthusiastic survive. Look at Richard Branson. When he started out in business back in the 1960s there was little to suggest that command and control was crumbling, certainly not in the corporate world. By discarding hierarchical power in favour of inspirational leadership, Branson was 25 years ahead of his time.

virtual visit   **www.virgin.com**

One of the characteristics of the Branson entrepreneurial style is knowing when to get out of the way and let people get on with it. The way that Virgin is structured means he really has no choice. With up to 200 companies in the Virgin family, it simply isn't feasible to think you could be hands-on boss of all of them. Whether by luck or design, then, Branson is forced to be a back-seat leader. (The one company that he doesn't seem able to leave alone is Virgin Atlantic.)

By and large, though, the hands-off leadership style is highly beneficial. Managers in the group enjoy the opportunity of running their own show; they find it highly motivating. Unlike most companies, too, they don't waste time on unnecessary meetings and pointless reports to give corporate headquarters something to do. This is because there are fewer than 25 people based in the Virgin head office, including Branson himself.

So if he isn't running the business on a day-to-day basis, what does Virgin's back-seat leader actually do? It's hard to describe exactly. You could say he enthuses other people, contributing to the buzz that emanates from every part of the group.

Beyond that, Branson is also important as a figurehead for the company. He puts his full support behind new ventures. The publicity he generates promotes all of the companies in the group. These days, he has to ration his personal appearances to one or two media events per business per year.

But there is something more to the Branson gen e model. He stands for something that makes people feel good to work for his company, a set of values that is important to Virgin employees. It's hard to pin down exactly what those values are, but they have something to do with running a business for a purpose other than purely profit. Another vital aspect of Branson's role is that of planning the future. Unlike business visionaries such as Bill Gates and Intel's Andy Grove, however, he is not in the business of crystal ball gazing or strategizing. Rather, Branson is a prospector, panning the multitude of business prospects that Virgin attracts for nuggets of purest gold. He is always on the lookout for new business ventures. He and his two expert advisers consider somewhere close to fifty proposals a week. Most will be rejected out of hand, but if there is a gleam of an opportunity for a new Virgin company they will take a long hard look.

It is one thing to recognize potential for a business, however, and quite another to make it a reality. But this is one of Branson's secrets: the ability to make things happen. He is the catalyst that triggers a chain reaction which transforms potential energy in a project or idea into kinetic energy that sends people scurrying in a thousand directions.

When the business consultant Don Cruickshank was brought in as group managing director to prepare Virgin to go public, he quickly realized that trying to get Branson to fit into a conventional organizational structure was pointless – and would be self-defeating. Instead, he sensibly concluded, the company would have to be structured around its energetic chairman.

Recognizing his talent for enthusing others, the ex-McKinsey consultant encouraged Branson to 'continue to dream up new ideas, to look at a bewildering array of new ventures and to start more companies in two years than most entre-preneurs do in their whole careers'.[23]

Branson should not try to alter his nature, Cruickshank warned. Instead he should stick to what he is really good at: motivating others and passing on his contagious enthusiasm that every new project would succeed. In short, Branson should devote all his energy to acting as a catalyst. All that was needed was a corps of people to tidy up behind him and to help him clarify what he was trying to achieve.

One of Branson's great talents is getting people all fired up about a new business idea and then letting them loose on it. His own enthusiasm is conta-gious, focusing excitement on a goal or destination, which then allows him to step back and let others run with it. Somehow, too, he spurs people on to achieve-ments they wouldn't have believed possible.

When you get right down to it, Richard Branson has no clearly defined business skill or training. He's not really a numbers man – he failed his elementary maths examination three times. Nor is he an IT whiz-kid – he doesn't know how to switch on a laptop, let alone design an operating system. Marketing and publicity he has a flair for, but he has little grasp of or interest in the theory behind them, preferring to do it his way. What then does Branson bring to the party (apart from the party itself)?

'What I do best is finding people and letting them work,' he says. 'Virgin staff are not mere hired hands. They are not managerial pawns in some gigantic chess game. They are entrepreneurs in their own right.'[24]

Of course, this can get out of hand. We are not naïve enough to argue that high octane energy and boundless enthusiasm don't have their downsides. Managing Richard Branson would be hellish. Having him as your boss would be hellish, but inspiring. There are a lot of enthusiastic bankrupts. There is a catch-22 here. 'Obsession doesn't guarantee success. On the other hand a lack of obsession does guarantee failure,' wrote Tom Peters in *Liberation Management*.[25] In this hyper-competitive era, obsession is a managerial necessity, but a potentially dangerous one.

It depends what entrepreneurs obsess about. In the business world, obsession takes on many different guises. Managers obsessed about their sales targets; obsessed with reengineering; obsessed with corporate politics; or obsessed with their latest great idea for boosting performance. And, more questionably, there are the managers obsessed with tidy desks, car parking spaces and the company's consumption of paperclips.

> Enthusiasm and energy bordering on obsession can open doors

Enthusiasm and energy bordering on obsession can open doors. Take Victor Kiam, the man who famously liked the company so much he bought it. In his biography, Kiam says: 'Business is a game and eight hours don't afford you enough time to score the deciding run.' As a youthful and obsessive salesman, Kiam stalked the USA seeking out every advantage possible. 'When a snowstorm hit my region it wasn't an obstacle: it was an opportunity! It was amazing how receptive a buyer could be when the snow outside his door was waist deep and climbing, and you were the only friendly face he had seen all day.' In business, such obsessiveness is not a curious foible. Often it is not even regarded as strange or unhealthy. People don't lose their jobs for being workaholics or devoting every moment of their lives to meeting sales targets.

And it can also set new standards of customer service. Companies such as McDonald's and Virgin are built round an obsessive commitment to giving customers quality service. McDonald's founder, Ray Kroc, used to pick up litter from car parks and was discovered one Saturday morning cleaning the muck out of the holes on a mop bucket with a toothbrush. The crew handbook which all

McDonald's workers receive lists strict dress codes based on hygiene consider-
ations and is prefaced by the words 'Cleanliness is like a magnet drawing
customers to McDonald's'. This is where enthusiasm, energy and a willingness to
distil business to its essentials shape entire organizations – positively, construc-
tively and profitably. The trouble is that, taken too far, obsession can blind
individuals or the organization to the warning signs suggesting that change is
required.

people people

The sixth important element in gen e DNA is that they value the human dimension; e = empathy. Previous generations just paid lip service to the idea. Gen e know that people make the difference. Despite their short-term career intentions, they still express loyalty to their managers, clients and organizations. However, their greatest commitment is to their immediate colleagues and staff. Gen e are people people.

e = empathy

Vital to this, in the technological age, is clear and effective communication. Sustaining high quality communication at all times is integral to gen e's management style. Without clear communication, good ideas disappear into the corporate ether. Communication is still about people. 'Despite the international-ization of markets, despite air travel, despite information technology, there are still things that are done best by people who find themselves frequently in the same room,' says economist guru John Kay.[26]

Sustaining high quality communication at all times is integral to gen e's management style

The changes that Percy Barnevik introduced at ABB in the 1990s were driven by simple, evocative communication. ABB continually states, communicates and evolves clear values. The ABB values – meeting customer needs, decentralization, taking action, respecting an ethic and cooperating – were reinforced through intensive in-house programmes of executive education, in which Barnevik and other members of the top management team invested a great deal of time. The prime values, from Barnevik's point of view, were meeting customer needs and decentralization. ABB emphasized human contact – what Barnevik's successor Goran Lindahl has labelled 'human engineering'.

> Gen e have a capacity endlessly to regurgitate their message with total dedication and not a hint of boredom

Gen e have a capacity endlessly to regurgitate their message with total dedication and not a hint of boredom. The great business leaders – and that is what some of gen e are set to become – know the value of repetition. They can recite their business bite, their high concept, time and time again. 'There is a certain amount of showmanship. They play their roles to perfection. They stand in the middle of their strategy. They don't preach the strategy; they are the strategy. They communicate consistently and continually. They repeat the same messages again and again. It is like advertising. But they never grow tired of saying it – there is no sign of boredom, no cynicism, no sarcasm.

> This appetite for communication is clearly linked to a more humane style of management. The people deserve to be told and it is your job to tell them

They give words real meaning,' says Jan Lapidoth, who worked alongside the legendary SAS CEO Jan Carlzon and now heads the Customer Focus Institute in Stockholm. This appetite for communication is clearly linked to a more humane style of management. The people deserve to be told and it is your job to tell them.

emotional economics

N ow the going becomes soft: e = emotion. 'There is money in emotion. This is not an obscure flaky agenda. It may represent the antithesis to the previous commercial rationale but it is not anti-commercialism. It is the new commercialism. It is not

$e = emotion$

flaky – it is funky. Poetry and profits need not be mutually exclusive. If contemporary business was only a case of bits, brains and brands – why does Citibank work with Elton John? Why did Motorola and Microsoft team up with the Rolling Stones? And why did Miller enter an alliance with MC Hammer? The answer is short

www.funkybusiness.com | **virtual visit**

and melodic: vibes,' observe Kjell Nordström and Jonas Ridderstråle in *Funky Business*.[27] Nordström and Ridderstråle have also coined the phrase 'economies of soul'.

Emotional economics rule. 'People have an enormous need for art and poetry that industry does not yet understand,' says Alberto Alessi, founder of the eponymous company. Emotion affects every business everywhere. Listen to a head designer at Ford: 'In the past we tended to focus inwardly, looking for functional efficiency. Now the mindshift is to more outwardly focused, emotional satisfaction for the consumer.'[28]

Emotions and the notion of Emotional Intelligence (EQ) are integral to gen e. They believe that the ability of managers to understand and manage their own emotions and those of the people they work with is the key to better business performance.

The emotional bible is Daniel Goleman's (1995) book *Emotional Intelligence*.[29] Rising rates of aggression and depression in US schools instigated Goleman's far-reaching research. He concluded that human competencies like self-awareness, self-discipline, persistence and empathy are of greater consequence than IQ in much of life. Goleman asserted that we ignore the emotional competencies at our peril and that children can – and should – be taught these abilities at school.

> Emotions and the notion of Emotional Intelligence (EQ) are integral to gen e. They believe that the ability of managers to understand and manage their own emotions and those of the people they work with is the key to better business performance

Goleman, a psychologist by training, built on the ideas of the Harvard-based psychologist Howard Gardner – credited with the development of the multiple intelligence theory – and the Yale psychologist Peter Salovey. In his book, he adopts Salovey's definition of emotional intelligence. According to Salovey, EQ can be observed in five key areas:

● knowing one's emotions

● managing emotions

● motivating oneself

● recognizing emotions in others

● handling relationships.

Goleman has gone on to explore the issue of personal and professional effectiveness. In a business world too often obsessed by cold analysis and intellect, he argues, the emotional climate is more important to the success of an organization than previously recognized. Goleman's (1998) book, *Working With Emotional Intelligence*, argues that workplace competencies based on emotional intelligence play a far greater role in star performance than do intellect or technical skill, and that both individuals and companies will benefit from cultivating these capabilities.[30]

In particular, Goleman claims, the emotional dimension is critical in determining the effectiveness of leaders; he argues that in demanding jobs where above average IQ is a given, superior emotional capability gives leaders an edge. At senior levels, emotional rather than rational intelligence marks out the true leader. According to Goleman, studies of outstanding performers in organizations show that about two-thirds of the abilities that set star performers apart in the leadership stakes are based on emotional intelligence; only one-third of the skills that matter relate to raw intelligence (as measured by IQ) and technical expertise.

> Studies of outstanding performers in organizations show that about two-thirds of the abilities that set star performers apart in the leadership stakes are based on emotional intelligence

'Our emotions are hardwired into our being,' he explains. 'The very architecture of the brain gives feelings priority over thought.' In reality, it is impossible entirely to separate thought from emotion. 'We can be effective only when the two systems – our emotional brain and our thinking brain – work together. That working relationship, which encompasses most of what we do in life, is the essence of emotional intelligence.'

Gen e is the first group of business people who forcefully endorse these findings. Their insights, perceptions and management styles are grounded on emotions as much as on rational analysis. They are as likely to reach for a book on *feng shui* as to draw a two-by-two matrix.

Emotional economics are already impacting organizations. 'We're talking about "relationship savvy",' notes Gill Stringer, executive development manager at BT. 'That's how you inspire people. We're looking to develop interpersonal sensitivity and a mindset that is about collaboration, and understanding what others have to contribute, and seeing partnerships as an opportunity to learn.'[31]

During 1999 BT went through a major rethink of the leadership profile required to support the company's global

www.bt.com   **virtual visit**

ambitions and the new leadership profile was presented to the main board. 'Our strategy for global expansion includes a high degree of partnering and joint ventures. As boundaries get fuzzier and fuzzier, leadership becomes more and more vital. It's always been a big issue, but the requirements have changed. We don't want people who will sit at the top of their organizational pyramid and say "I manage what I control, and I control what I manage." The emphasis is on relationship management,' notes Gill Stringer. 'The critical issue is interpersonal sensitivity. This ties in with emotional intelligence. These issues are converging now for us not because they are nice to do, but because they are being driven by business objectives. We are moving to a more holistic approach.'

The good news, according to Goleman, is that emotional intelligence can be learned. There are five dimensions:

1   *Self-awareness:* we seldom pay attention to what we feel. A stream of moods runs in parallel to our thoughts. This and previous emotional experiences provide a context for our decision making.

2   *Managing emotions:* all effective leaders learn to manage their emotions, especially the big three – anger, anxiety, sadness. This is a decisive life skill.

3   *Motivating others:* the root meaning of motive is the same as the root of emotion – to move.

4   *Showing empathy:* the flip side of self-awareness is the ability to read emotions in others.

5   *Staying connected:* emotions are contagious. There is an unseen transaction that passes between us in every interaction that makes us feel either a little better or a little worse. Goleman calls this a 'secret economy'. It holds the key to motivating the people we work with.

As gen e's impact deepens, this secret economy will be brought out into the open. Emotional economics will be acknowledged as commercial reality.

making a difference

Gen e trait no. 8: e = ethics. For gen e financial motivation is limited. Truly. They are not angelic figures who regard financial rewards as unimportant. They expect to be well rewarded, but look beyond the narrow motivation of money alone.

e = ethics

We are not suggesting that gen e are a pushover. They want a share of the action. No effort without equity. Forget the $1,000 bonus if the project works out, let's talk ownership. Through its employee stock options scheme, Microsoft is said to have created 21,000 millionaires. Ownership is one of Amazon's six stated core values.

> We are not suggesting that gen e are a pushover. They want a share of the action. No effort without equity

'Venture capitalists are backing new start-ups with cheap finance and have such faith in these new enterprises they are allowing the people running them to keep large parcels of share options,' notes a recent PricewaterhouseCoopers report. 'Dot.com directors are accepting low salaries in return for the chance to become seriously rich if their company is listed. Incumbent companies have neither the advantage of low-cost finance nor that of low-cost expertise. They must borrow capital or retain profits to enter the Web sector and must pay top prices to the people running their e-businesses. This wipes out some or all of the increases in market share or efficiency that they gain through Web-based commerce. This, in turn, is reflected in reduced market valuations.'[32]

> Affecting lives in a positive way is what the leaders we studied and talked to thought it was all about. They believe in what they are doing or trying to achieve

Affecting lives in a positive way is what the leaders we studied and talked to thought it was all about. They believe in what they are doing or trying to achieve. It sounds corny, but has anyone ever done a good job if they weren't committed to doing it? Perhaps once, but not day after day.

Paul Allen, Microsoft founder, recalling the day he and Bill Gates realized they had shipped 1,000,000 copies of BASIC, says: 'We were marveling that, wow, a million people were using our code to do God-knows-what number of interesting things. That was such a gratifying thing to realize, that you have been able to affect other people's lives in a positive way.'[33]

> Affecting lives is what drives gen e. They reject many of the old views of capitalism. They don't buy the greed is good attitude of the 1980s

Affecting lives is what drives gen e. They reject many of the old views of capitalism. They don't buy the greed is good attitude of the 1980s. Money-grabbing opportunism masqueraded as entrepreneurialism in the 1980s. Little of lasting value was built at this time – though a great deal was destroyed, driven by the demonic drumbeat of market forces. Gen e are creators not destroyers. Instead, they are more in step with social change – placing a higher value on the social impact of business. People have been bemoaning the destruction of the planet and other issues since the 1960s; gen e actually want to do something about it. Social entrepreneurs are active in the not-for-profit sector.

> Gen e are creators not destroyers

Liam Black, for example, is CEO of the Furniture Resource Centre in Liverpool, England, a not-for-profit organization that sells reconditioned furniture to a variety of customers. Under Black's leadership, the organization has received plaudits for its entrepreneurial activities. For example, it recently pitched for and won a contract for the disposal of unwanted household refuge in the city – including unwanted furniture.

virtual visit   **www.frc.mersinet.co.uk**

Through the deft recycling of items destined for the trash heap, Black has proved that money can be made out of nothing. 'We have demonstrated that entrepreneurial behaviour is just as relevant for the charitable sector as it is for the private sector,' says Black.

Gen e want more than just a pay cheque at the end of the month. They want meaning and purpose. They want to change the world. Since the early days, Amazon.com has had the stated aim of revolutionizing business. Staff are encouraged to join the e-commerce crusade. Nine-to-fivers need not apply. The company sees its mission as changing both how people shop and how they think about shopping. Employees are offered the opportunity not just to make money but to make history, by making the cyberstore a success.

> Gen e want more than just a pay cheque at the end of the month. They want meaning and purpose. They want to change the world

Pierre Omidyar, founder of eBay.com, the online auction company, is another man with a mission. 'What I wanted to do was create a marketplace where everyone has access to the same information,' he says. 'The first commercial efforts were from larger companies

www.e.bay.com　　**virtual visit**

that were saying "Gee, we can use the internet to sell stuff to people." Clearly, if you're coming from a democratic, libertarian point of view, having corporations just cram more products down people's throats doesn't seem like a lot of fun. I really wanted to give the individual the power to be the producers as well.'

Linked to this are two other issues. First, there is the growing importance of values. Some companies have long recognized the importance of values to the motivation of staff. The pharmaceuticals company Merck, for example, has a track record of recognizing the importance of placing meaning and morality above pure profits. Mectizan was a drug designed to combat onchocerciasis – known as 'river blindness'. River blindness is caused when a water-borne parasitic worm enters the body and making its way through the body ends up in the eyes where it causes irreparable damage leading to blindness. This disease is particularly prevalent in third world countries, afflicting over a million people.

Merck recognized that while this was potentially a large market, it was not a wealthy one, with the majority of end users unable to afford the product. However, the company pressed on with the drug's development and production, hoping that government agencies or other bodies would step forward to buy the product. In the event none did. What did Merck do? It gave the drug away, free to all who needed it. It also helped distribute the product, ensuring it reached those who needed it.

> Gen e are especially
> concerned about values

When asked why Merck did what they did, the company's CEO replied that not to have done so could have demoralized scientists who worked for a company expressly in the business of 'preserving and improving human life'.

Gen e are especially concerned about values. Some companies now recognize this fact to retain gen e staff. Founded in 1984 by Bernie Vonderschmitt and Ross Freeman, for example, the Silicon Valley based semiconductor company Xilinx has always favoured a respectful 'non-confrontational culture' over an aggressive one. The challenge has been keeping it that way and still conducting business effectively.

virtual visit **www.xilinx.com**

As Nancy Nadler, HRD manager, observes, 'If you've been to any of the big semiconductor companies you know that people yell a lot. You have to have a thick skin. Xilinx had a different culture from the very beginning. It's what makes us different, what attracts really good people here. It's what keeps them here. It doesn't mean we don't work hard or that we don't have tough deadlines.'

Over time, however, the company strayed from the unstated values of the founders. In particular, the non-confrontational culture threatened to undermine effectiveness. In 1995 the company thrashed out some explicit values: the result – a list of eight values forming the acronym CREATIVE:

- **C** ustomer-focused
- **R** espect
- **E** xcellence
- **A** ccountability
- **T** eam work

- **I** ntegrity
- **V** ery open communication
- **E** njoying our work.

Significantly, accountability was made into an explicit value. This exercise has helped the company and its employees focus on the important issues.

In an employee video explaining the values, CEO Wim Roelandts went so far as to say, 'If these values are foreign to you then you are not going to be comfortable here. We are not going to fire you but, over time, you will not feel at home.'

In their book *Built to Last*, James C. Collins and Jerry Porras[34] studied the factors that characterized companies which were successful over many years. A set of core values, they found, provided continuity and a sense of identity. These companies place their values above profit maximization. Yet research suggests that they outperform companies that put profits first, providing a better return to their shareholders over time. The companies identified by Collins and Porras, for example, had outperformed the general stock market by a factor of 12 since 1925.

> Gen e are acutely aware of what they will one day leave behind. The notion of corporate legacy extends business beyond the here and now

More recently, Arie de Geus looked at corporate longevity in his book *The Living Company*.[35] De Geus writes about the managers of long-lived companies: 'They succeeded through the generational flow of members, and considered themselves stewards of the longstanding enterprise. Each management generation was only a link in a long chain.'

Second, there is the realization that businesspeople should be measured on what they create rather than simply financial results (important though these obviously are). Gen e are acutely aware of what they will one day leave behind. The notion of corporate legacy extends business beyond the here and now. It raises the issue of what one generation of management should pass on to the next. In any long-lived company, generations of CEOs will preside over the culture of the organization, inheriting it from their predecessor, passing it on to their successor.

Some organizations go to remarkable lengths to preserve their distinctive cultures and safeguard their corporate legacies. Merrill Lynch, for example, has its five 'Principles' engraved on plaques lining the corridors of its world headquarters. Johnson and Johnson has its values written down in a book – the 'Credo' – which dates back to the founding fathers of the company. Hewlett-Packard has the H-P Way, which employees write out by hand and pin up next to the picture of their family.

> Stewardship is an idea that is increasingly relevant to business

Stewardship is an idea that is increasingly relevant to business. How successive leaders deal with this corporate legacy is rarely discussed. It goes beyond traditional ideas of succession planning – deciding to whom the baton will be passed and developing the next generation of managers; or even the work on corporate memory carried out by the American management writer Art Kleiner.[36]

The idea of corporate legacy asserts that senior management is the custodian of the values that underpin the culture, conserving them on behalf and for the benefit of the company in the future. It goes right to the heart and soul of the business: what it exists for and the values it holds most dear.

This is particularly critical when the founder or founders of a company hand over control. What marks out the great CEOs from the rest is their ability to ensure that the company goes on after them. Bill Gates and Richard Branson are both great leaders in their own right, but what legacy will they leave behind?

There is another critical dimension to the legacy issue. As economic conditions change with the passage of time, there is often pressure within companies to deviate from the values, drop them altogether or take on new ones. The question that then has to be answered is whether values can change, be replaced – or are they sacrosanct?

Opinion varies on this point. 'Our basic principles have endured intact since our founders conceived them,' said John Young, former CEO of Hewlett-Packard in 1992. 'We distinguish between core values and practices; core values don't change, but the practices might.'

Writing in *Fortune* magazine, Thomas A. Stewart draws a different conclusion: 'Over time self-interest distorts corporate values ... To bring them back, top management must constantly reiterate, refresh, reinterpret and rename.'

If the original sense of the values has been lost, if the values have evolved in the wrong direction, it is the top team's role to redefine and reinterpret the values so that they are relevant. Cadbury-Schweppes is one company that has tackled this issue. Today, the soft drinks and food giant distributes its branded products in more than 200 countries, but it can trace its history back to the 1800s when John Cadbury first started selling tea and coffee in Birmingham, England. During the 1970s, Cadbury faced a period of transition following its merger with Schweppes. In 1976 Sir Adrian Cadbury, then chairman, took steps to ensure that the Cadbury values would be permanently enshrined in the new company's culture.

The Cadbury values were printed in a document 'The Character of the Company'. They include a commitment to: competitive ability, quality, clear objectives, simplicity, openness and responsibility to stakeholders. These values have helped Cadbury-Schweppes maintain its position in a changing world. It is a legacy that has been handed down.

Gen e reject short-term thinking and, despite the apparently overwhelming demands of the present, nurture their legacy from the date of their very first business plan. The future is theirs as well as the present.

the ad men

St. Luke's is the ad agency behind the UK government's £18 million ($29.7 million) Welfare to Work campaign. With its own distinctive approach to the ad business it is challenging the way companies think not just about advertising but about the fundamentals of running a business. It is gen e ethics at work in a setting where, stereotypically at least, ethical dilemmas are few and far between.

In a previous life, St. Luke's was the London office of the California-based Chiat/Day agency. Along with Saatchi and Saatchi and WPP, Chiat/Day skilfully rode the advertising wave of the 1980s. St. Luke's chairman Andy Law and CEO Dave Abraham grew up in the hey-day of the 1980s-style super-agency. By 1994, however, they had become disenchanted with the West Coast agency. When it was announced that Chiat/Day was to merge with another agency, TBWA, they decided to jump ship, taking the entire 35-strong London office with them.

Since then, St. Luke's has set out its stall as a new sort of ad agency, one that is underpinned by ethical concerns. It's a brave step. Some people will no doubt question its sincerity. Advertising – St. Luke's style – elevates the position of marketing executive to a sort of moral champion. 'We are a conviction company,' Abraham says. 'We believe in our clients' products.'

The company also believes in new ways of working. Staff at the Euston-based agency have no desks of their own. Between meetings they hot-desk – taking a seat at any one of the computer stations they share communally. Telephones are radio based and small enough to fit into a pocket. Calls follow employees from place to place. When the pressure becomes too much they can hang out in the staff 'chill out room'.

virtual visit   **www.stlukes.co.uk**

Themed rooms are big at St. Luke's. Client meetings are held in 'brand rooms'. Once a client signs up with the agency, they are allocated a conference room that is fitted out in the style and culture of the brand, which they can use whenever they choose, calling on St. Luke's staff as required. So, for example, a room set aside for Boots No. 17 make-up range is furnished with its target teenage buyer in mind, complete with bunk beds and posters of pop stars on the walls.

According to Andy Law: 'The aim is to operate in the "creative age" rather than the "industrial age". It's all about being comfortable with chaotic, almost anarchic, ways of working which frees employees to be creative and to work in a "non-linear way".'

Underpinning its management philosophy is a new sort of corporate structure which could be the blueprint for the future. The company is completely employee owned, with staff given a further equal equity stake in the business at the end of each year. This is not the usual token distribution of shares. Every one of the company's one hundred or so employees – from the creative director to the switchboard operator – receives equal shares. In many ways, it is a reaction to the excesses of the 1980s.

Andy Law is critical of the way many advertising agencies are run, with senior management taking the lion's share of the profits from the creativity and ideas of younger staff. 'There are a lot of greedy people in the advertising business,' says Law. 'The industry is driven by ego. By and large it does not respect its employees.'

Wary of the avarice of the classic pyramid ad agency model, St. Luke's was created with a cooperative structure called a Qualifying Employee Shareholder Trust – or QUEST. It is run by a trust – which owns 25 per cent of the shares. The remainder is divided equally among the employees.

The company's affairs are governed not by the traditional board of directors but by a six-member council. By law one member must be a lawyer; the other five trustees are democratically elected by staff. The new way of working is part and parcel of a different approach to the ad business. David Abraham, St. Luke's other co-creator and CEO, believes it's time advertising grew up.

'In a lot of advertising consumers are asked to live in almost a fantasy world,' he says. 'What we're saying is let's try to make it closer to reality. All companies exist in a social context; it's time we recognized that fact.'

> Many people regard advertising as the cynical manipulation of public taste. St. Luke's wants to change all that

Many people regard advertising as the cynical manipulation of public taste. St. Luke's wants to change all that. It aims to move advertising from a fantasy world to something which resonates with people's lives. Abraham and Law believe that runs deeper than promoting stereotypes of 1990s man and woman.

Winning the account for Welfare to Work, the centrepiece of UK Chancellor Gordon Brown's New Deal for unemployed youngsters, was a huge coup for St. Luke's and an opportunity to put its own style of advertising on the map. In the television ads, real businessmen leap out of their seats on the train to proclaim the New Deal. They are met with the sort of edgy suspicion from other passengers familiar to commuters everywhere.

For years, advertising executives have had a bad press on both sides of the Atlantic. A 1995 Gallup poll, for example, asked Americans to rank more than twenty different occupations in terms of honesty and ethics. The only jobs to score lower than advertising executives were members of Congress and secondhand car salesmen.

It is that legacy which St. Luke's hopes to free itself from. Clearly, its ethical approach was in tune with the caring–sharing 1990s. But Andy Law insists it is not about being politically correct for its own sake. 'St. Luke's is not the "nicey, nicey advertising agency",' he says. 'Good advertising is provocative sometimes. But we do believe all organizations should conduct themselves ethically.'

'At the end of the day, are we still trying to sell more stuff?' asks David Abraham. 'The answer is yes.'

direct action

Next time you drink a cup of tea or coffee spare a thought for the farmer whose crop produced it. Better still, take a look at the label on the packet. It could tell you whether you are a responsible global citizen or party to the exploitation of third world producers.

Cafédirect, founded in 1991 in response to the collapse of world coffee prices in 1989, grew out of a wildly ambitious initiative launched by four charitable organizations – Oxfam, Twin Trading, Traidcraft and Equal Exchange. Cafédirect was created by the Fairtrade Foundation, and the success of the Fairtrade consumer label represents an important change in the business landscape and one which gen e is a powerful force in pushing forward. The fairtrade mark is a guarantee to consumers that the products they are purchasing directly support third world producers and guarantee them a fair deal.

> The success of the Fairtrade consumer label represents an important change in the business landscape and one which gen e is a powerful force in pushing forward

www.fairtrade.co.uk `virtual visit`

Though not a charity, cafédirect has a unique set of guiding principles, which are backed by its shareholders – the four founding organizations. The company's philosophy is to deliver a better deal to coffee growers in developing countries, while also delivering the best coffee to consumers. It set out to address three key problems facing coffee growers in a notoriously cut-throat market:

- world price volatility
- rip-off middlemen
- the high cost of local capital for investment.

When it was launched, the concept of a 100 per cent Fairtrade business was dismissed by many as unfeasible. The brand was originally sold in church halls and the like, until the company badgered the supermarket chain Safeway into trialing it at some of its stores.

The cafédirect brand now commands a 4 per cent share of the roast and ground coffee market and a 2 per cent share of the freeze-dried instant coffee market. Its products are sold at checkouts in 90 per cent of UK supermarkets.

Fairtrade is the embodiment of the caring–sharing element in the make-up of gen e. The Fairtrade Foundation focuses on small growers who are vulnerable to middlemen. Buyers like cafédirect purchase directly from producer cooperatives which are registered with the Fairtrade Labelling Organization (FLO). Key to this is the creation of long-term relationships with growers. Farmers receive a fair price for the crops they produce, which does not drop below a decent minimum regardless of how low the world price falls. They are also offered access to credit at reasonable rates, allowing for investment.

The company works with Fairtrade-certified smallholder farmer cooperatives and other producer organizations across the major tea and coffee growing regions of the world. It has partnerships with 16 coffee cooperatives in Latin America and Africa spanning eight countries including Mexico and Peru. Teadirect, the company's other product stream, is sourced from four grower partnerships in Uganda and Tanzania.

The business model is simple. Buying direct from the smallholder cooperatives allows the company to cut out middlemen, offering a better price to the growers. In turn, the growers provide only their very best quality crops. The company also pays an additional 10 per cent 'social premium' to growers.

Surveys have consistently shown that consumers are prepared to pay a bit more to ensure third world producers are not exploited. A 1996 Gallup survey found that 60 per cent of consumers 'would make every effort to buy Fairtrade products wherever possible'; and 60 per cent of shoppers said they are willing to boycott products or stores on ethical grounds. A recent NOP survey found that 85 per cent of people 'would like to see fairly traded products in their super-market'.

The success of Cafédirect suggests that consumers are prepared to put their wallets where their principles are. Sales of Fairtrade products are growing by an average of 65 per cent per annum (the total value of these goods sold at checkouts exceeded £14 million ($23.1 million) in 1999).

> The success of Cafédirect suggests that consumers are prepared to put their wallets where their principles are

Its success is also a sign that the rules of business are changing. Ethical trading used to mean not breaking the law or in some way misleading, deceiving or endangering people or the environment. That is no longer the case. Consumer interest in ethical issues is moving the goalposts for companies.

In recent years a number of household brands, including the sports apparel company Nike, have found themselves in deep water over allegations of exploitation in third world countries. But while Nike and others have had to mend their ways in the face of consumer protests, cafédirect has demonstrated that it is possible to build a business on the principle of fair trade.

the art of balance

$e = equilibrium$

The ninth habit of highly effective members of gen e is the quest to find a new balance between work and family;. e = equilibrium. Gen e don't see it as an either/or. They want it all. Generation X were labelled as slackers. But gen e are anything but. Achieving work–life balance is one of the greatest challenges these people face. In one survey, some 94 per cent said they were willing to work long hours if they had to but, interestingly, nearly a fifth would like to work part-time (men and women); and 40 per cent would like more choice over working hours.

'When I'm old, looking back, I want to be able to say I have led an extraordinary life,' says a young MBA currently working for a credit card company. 'My goal is to have been extremely happy. To squeeze life for everything it can offer. Work will play a big part … but it isn't everything. There are so many things I want to do – to climb mountains, to travel, to learn to sail, to give something back to others, to spend time with my friends and family … and to slow down frequently enough to keep healthy and balanced. How can I fit everything in?' Good question – though we reflect, brutally, that the answer may not easily be found at a credit card company.

On this point we are not utterly convinced. Gen e talk a great deal about achieving a balance in their lives. They talk of what they really want to do. Often, however, work takes over. The route to personal fulfilment and an 'interesting life' is blocked by meetings with venture capitalists.

One obvious measure of this is working hours. 'I personally work long hours, but not as long as I used to,' Bill Gates observed recently. 'I certainly haven't expected other people to work as hard as I did. Most days I don't work more than 12 hours. On weekends I rarely work more than 8 hours. There are weekends I take off and I take vacations.'[37] Not much room for a life, then.

When it comes to working hours Americans work the longest hours in the industrialized world. The average American worker clocks up nearly 2,000 hours at work every year. Despite the heady speed of technological innovation, American working hours have actually increased by 4 per cent since 1980.[38] The USA fares badly compared to a wide range of nations. Norwegian workers work an average of 1,399 hours per year, while Japanese workers work nearly two weeks less than their American counterparts. The general trend is downwards. German hours have fallen from 1,742 to 1,560 between the 1980s and the late 1990s. At the same time as workers in Europe have been working fewer hours, productivity has actually been rising. Indeed, productivity growth of 22 per cent in western Europe since 1980 exceeds that experienced in the USA.

The USA leads the rankings in terms of GDP per person, but plummets to ninth if measured by GDP per hour. Japan similarly drops from third to eighteenth. Meanwhile, Belgium moves from tenth to first. 'Americans have more money because they have less leisure,' MIT's Lester Thurow has simply noted.

Wealth has increased. Over 3.5 million US households have a net worth of $1 million or above. Yet over 17 million Americans suffer from depression and over 22 million take 'mood-lifting drugs'. 'People are reaching the top, using all of their

> When it comes to working hours Americans work the longest hours in the industrialized world. The average American worker clocks up nearly 2,000 hours at work every year

> Over 17 million Americans suffer from depression and over 22 million take 'mood-lifting drugs'

means to get money, power, and glory – and then self-destructing,' Harriet Rubin writes. 'Perhaps they never wanted success in the first place, or didn't like what they saw when they finally achieved it.'[39]

This is not just an American thing. A five-year tracking study by the UK's Institute of Management and the University of Manchester Institute of Science and Technology found that the work and home life balance was still a pipe dream. Over 80 per cent of execs worked over 40 hours a week and one in ten worked over 60 hours. A resounding – though depressing – 86 per cent said that the long hours had an effect on their relationship with their children and 71 per cent said that it damaged their health.[40]

'We want to have it all: more money – and more time. More success – a more satisfying family life. More creature comforts – and more sanity. We can work hard, we can find love and have a family, and we can enjoy the fruits of our success,' concludes a survey in *Fast Company*. Equilibrium is proving elusive – even for gen e.

> Equilibrium is proving elusive – even for gen e

cake eating

Some pull it off. Equilibrium, when found, comes in many shapes and forms. The quest for balance leads gen e in a variety of directions. Not all rush out and start their own business while busily cutting the corporate umbilical cord. Dual careering – an ugly phrase, we know – is increasingly common as people try to crowd entrepreneurial activities into already busy executive lives.

> Equilibrium, when found, comes in many shapes and forms. The quest for balance leads gen e in a variety of directions

Untrained in business theory, old style entrepreneurs busked it. They were outsiders. Uncomfortable with the existing rules, they invented their own. To them, the very notion of a professionally trained manager was anathema. To them, the suits of the business establishment were the enemy. 'Few entrepreneurs have business school qualifications and few stand out from the crowd in any way. In fact many start out with little or no experience of running a business and instead rely on common sense and learning along the way,' observes David Hall, author of *In the Company of Heroes*, a book on traditional entrepreneurs.[41]

Generation e are different. Many of them have done the corporate gig and got the T-shirt to prove it. But they found it too restrictive or simply too slow, so they've opted to go their own way. They are people like Dave Allan and Matt Kingdon, who left the cosy sinecure of Unilever to start the innovation consultancy ?What If!. They were joined by Kris Murrin, formerly of Procter and Gamble, and another ex-Unilever marketeer Daz Rudkin.

Generation e are different. Many of them have done the corporate gig and got the T-shirt to prove it

'When we first left our comfortable corporate jobs for a minimal wage and a single Apple Mac, people thought we were brave. They kept slapping us on the back and saying "Good luck guys, I wish I had your balls!" It wasn't like that for us. We simply had to live our dreams. We had always believed that we would run our own business and the time had come.'[42]

Dual careering supplies a little security for those who prefer to keep one foot in the corporate world and launch a business or two on the side. Take 35-year-old Gerry Griffin, for example. He combines a high-powered career in public relations with various entrepreneurial activities on the side. For four years at the London agency Fleishman Hillard, followed by two years as communications director at London Business School, he was recently Y2K guru at Burson Marsteller. That's the day job.

virtual visit **www.dotcon.com**

Gen e are natural multi-taskers

In his spare time, Griffin is still involved with managing the mushroom farm he started in Ireland in the late 1980s. Two years of mixing with academics at London Business School convinced him he was qualified to write business books. He now has two successful business titles to his name – .Con and The Power Game.[43] Gen e are natural multi-taskers.

One of the brightest ideas we have come across is that of Online Originals. It is a business built on one of those bright ideas which you wish you had thought of first. The company publishes books by unsung authors on the internet. You can browse through sample chapters at the company's site. Then, if you decide to buy, the book is sent to you electronically. The 36 books currently available include everything from Patricia le Roy's novel The Angels of Russia to the weighty Evolution in the Systems Age. All books cost £4 ($6) – of which the authors receive half. Readers can read the books on their palm pilots.

virtual visit **www.onlineoriginals.co.uk**

The people behind Online Originals are dual careerists David Gettman and his two partners, Doug Alexander and Christopher Macann. They launched Online Originals early in 1997. 'The publishing industry is dominated by three huge companies,' says Gettman. 'So, there is huge commercial pressure on publishers. They can't have loss leaders. They are scared of taking risks.'[44] Online Originals is making a mark with its mix of fiction and non-fiction. Books are available in French and English. German is soon to be added. Ideas and manuscripts are pouring in. The 16 original titles have mushroomed. Gettman and his partners are not quite new Michael Dells. So far, the venture pays expenses and little more. They all have proper jobs – Gettman is a communications consultant – and are willing to watch the business grow. 'We have a very valuable brand. Reading books in this way is foreign to many people,' says Gettman. 'It is a narrow field, but it will grow.' They might even have to leave their 'proper' jobs.

back to the lab

The final trait common to gen e is one of the simplest: e = experimentation. Try it. Fail. Then try something else. Implicit to the willingness of gen e to start young is a willingness to embrace failure. Gen e regard failure as a rite of passage. To them, it's a badge of advancement, proof of attainment. They know that all the great entrepreneurs have a failure at some time. You have to fail to succeed.

> e = experimentation

Gen e know that failure may just be around the next corner. The bigger the prize, the further there is to fall. The technological revolution is littered with 'nearly' men and women. In April 1981, Adam Osborne showed off the Osborne 1 computer for the first time. Sales flooded in and by September 1981 his company was recording monthly sales of

> To gen e, failure is a learning experience.

over $1 million. The Osborne 1 and Adam Osborne seemed to be at the forefront of the technological revolution. The confident and cheerfully opinionated Osborne appeared to be a man of his times. 'From brags to riches' read one magazine headline. It was a fleeting glimpse of what might have been. During 1982 Osborne Computer reported losses of $8 million. It was soon bankrupt, an historical footnote. To gen e, failure is a learning experience.

Fail and fail again. Gen e are natural risk takers. In this they take their lead from some older execs. 'Euro Disney gave us all a good glass of cold water to the face,' admits Disney's Michael Eisner, a seasoned leader with more than a hint of gen e in his DNA. 'There's not a meeting goes by that somebody doesn't say, "Ah, Euro Disney, Euro Disney. Can we afford to do this?" Okay, I've heard it. I can say we've learned. But I really do feel – about business and about life – that everybody has to make mistakes, it's okay. I have never wavered from the belief that I'm glad we did Euro Disney and that it is a monument to the creativity of our company. But there is a reality of life known as economics, which always comes into the equation no matter how many pyramids you want to climb.'[45]

> Gen e's willingness to take risks sits uncomfortably with corporate reality elsewhere. Caution rules

Fail and remember. Eisner has learned the value of failure. 'We had a generation of executives who had never been around failure. We had this momentum that never seemed to end. We were climbing this ladder that seemed to have no top. Even I got kind of used to it and comfortable with it,' he now admits, realizing that it is one thing having an infinite ladder but quite another when the rungs come to an abrupt halt.

'I tell people here that there are two possibilities – success and failure – but it's the possibility of both that creates the best results. Risk taking is fun when you succeed … but I don't know as much about the other side of the equation as I should,' says Bill Gates – he knows that failure provides learning if you allow it but is so frightened of failure that it drives him to success.[46]

Gen e's willingness to take risks sits uncomfortably with corporate reality elsewhere. Caution rules. 'Executives are uncomfortable with ambiguity and uncertainty because, we suspect, they appreciate at some level that ambiguity involves a kind of learning that they find uncomfortable. There is a real possibility that they could learn something that would be a major development if they were able to get to grips with the opportunity,' say leadership researchers Philip Hodgson and Randall White. 'If they were able to let go, they could take on something new, embrace something unpracticed. But it does involve a risk. The risks are: loss of face, perhaps admitting to themselves (as a perfectionist this is always difficult) that they might not be as good as they would like to appear.'

The message from gen e is to learn from failure. Shit happens. The CEO of a major US corporation hands out awards for Best Failures. Fail and learn. 'Most of the things I have learnt were not learned formally but through accidents and failure. I learned from small catastrophes,' admits Charles Handy, author of *The Age of Unreason*.[47] Handy is not alone. Most of us learn in such a haphazard and occasionally unhappy way. If there were awards for Best Failures we would have a large number to choose from.

> The message from gen e is to learn from failure. Shit happens

Indeed, one UK newspaper ran a weekly column entitled 'My Biggest Mistake'. It was riveting reading as manager after manager confessed to some appalling misjudgment. It was notable that all the mistakes were made in prehistoric times – the executives couldn't admit to recent errors of judgment – and that their vital lessons stayed with the executives. In many cases they haunted them. A mistake made was a lesson learned and remembered.

Trouble is, in organizations fear of failure becomes a survival instinct. We go into organizations and we learn and are taught by the organization how to operate. 'Fear of failure is the major blockage to developing skills for handling uncertainty. But if we are to maximize learning we have to re-orient ourselves to taking risks and making, perhaps creating, mistakes,' say Hodgson and White.

> Message: take risks together or take the biggest risk of all

Work at Decision Research, a company based in Eugene, Oregon, studying risk management strategies, suggests that people are more likely to accept risks that they perceive as voluntarily undertaken, controllable, understandable and equally distributed. Conversely, people are less willing to take on risks which they don't understand and which are unfairly distributed.[48] Message: take risks together or take the biggest risk of all.

persistence sucks

The story of James Dyson and his dual cyclone vacuum cleaner is the stuff of business legend. In true David and Goliath (and gen e) style, Dyson beat near bankruptcy to establish his factory in Malmesbury, Wiltshire, and become the UK market leader. Fifty-something Dyson is proof that gen e is ageless and that persistence pays off.

As with most overnight successes, it has been a long journey for Dyson. He invented the bagless dual cyclone vacuum cleaner in 1978, when flared trousers were in fashion the first time round. Five long years and 5,127 prototypes later, his idea became a working model. But it was another ten years before the product reached the market.

In between, Dyson tried to get backing from the leading manufacturers. It was an eye-opening introduction to the world of big business. One multinational company, he says, would only agree to meet him if he signed over the rights to anything he might reveal to them in advance. Another wanted to license the product but refused to put anything in writing, saying that he would have to 'trust' them.

Dyson very sensibly declined both offers. But his brush with the corporate world gave him important insights into the sort of management culture that prevailed in some large companies. He was determined that his own firm would be different.

When it was finally launched in 1993, from the coach house at the family home, Dyson's first product, the DC01 turned the UK market for upright cleaners on its head. Just 23 months after its launch, his invention became Britain's best-selling vacuum cleaner, overtaking sales of Hoover, Electrolux, Panasonic and Miele. It was followed in 1995 by the DC02, the company's cylinder cleaner, which achieved similar results.

The company now employs 1,050 staff and produces 10,000 of the eponymous cleaning machines every day. The brand has more than half of the UK market by value and about a third by volume. Profits have jumped from £200,000 in 1993 to £19 million.

Today, the distinctive yellow and grey vacuum cleaners are to be found in homes the length and breadth of the country. Other vacuum cleaners may still be referred to generically as 'Hoovers', but a Dyson is a Dyson.

virtual visit   www.dyson.com

The company's management style also stands out from the crowd. The UK factory operates according to principles laid down by its founder. Employees must follow two rules: no smoking and no ties. (Dyson once told the board of a company on America's East Coast that ties make you go deaf in your old age – 'Wearing a suit strait-jackets you,' he also says.)

> Employees must follow two rules: no smoking and no ties

Despite his success, Dyson remains wary of the corporate mindset. Memos are banned. According to Dyson, they are 'just a way of passing the buck'. He has an even lower opinion of e-mail. 'The graphics are so appalling I just can't get interested enough to read them,' he says.

> The company has a slogan that says: 'We should be human beings not business people'

To this day the company has a slogan that says: 'We should be human beings not business people.' Dyson employees do not wear suits and ties and many are recruited straight from university because their minds are open to new ideas and working methods. Half of the senior management is female, including the managing director Tracy Ebdon-Poole.

Hierarchy is frowned upon. Every new employee – as the former trade minister Richard Needham discovered when he joined the company as a non-executive director – spends the first day assembling one of the famous dual cyclone machines which they can then buy for £25 (they retail for between £180 and £250) and take home for their own use. Familiarity with the product, the company believes, means that employees are more committed.

Individuality is also a strong feature of the company's culture. Dyson employees are encouraged to be different as a matter of principle – it's part of what Dyson calls his anti-brilliance campaign. 'Very few people can be brilliant. And they are over-valued. It's much more exciting to be a pioneer. Be a bit whacko and you shake people up. And we all need shaking up.'

> Dyson employees are encouraged to be different as a matter of principle – it's part of what Dyson calls his anti-brilliance campaign

Talented people are also given responsibility at a young age. The marketing manager was appointed when just 23 years old, the head of engineering at 28, and the head of graphics at 27. The average age of Dyson employees is 25.

Product quality is jealously guarded. All final assembly is done by hand (except for a machine that applies the sealing tape to the packaged cardboard boxes ready for despatch). The Dyson Overnight Courier Service (DOCS) means that customers' cleaners are collected from their homes free of charge, repaired and returned the next day. The idea is that customers are buying not just a single product but a complete service.

As one might expect, research and development are also key to the Dyson philosophy: a quarter of the entire workforce are design engineers and the company is constantly striving to find better-working and better-looking designs. 'Design is not just about how something looks, but how it works,' James Dyson insists.

The company has also shown itself to be adept at design-led marketing – producing special edition models of its upmarket vacuum cleaners that command an additional price premium.

At the Dyson factory, everything from engineering, design, production and servicing is done under one roof – something the company believes encourages staff ideas and the cross-fertilization of activities. The company is currently working on a new product line – possibly a washing machine or dishwasher.

Dyson has already shown that he can do it once; why not again? 'What we have done, that nobody thought we could do, is to take on the multinationals and beat them in a very short space of time, which I hope gives other people heart.' Persistence sucks.

Persistence sucks

the new economy

the chicken and e

The world in which gen e operate is one which has experienced radical changes in a short space of time. In the rest of the book we will look at the emergent world which gen e has done so much to shape. In particular, we will look at the new world order in terms of the new economy; changes in power structures; changes in working lives and career patterns; and, finally, changes within organizations.

First, the much vaunted new economy. The skills of gen e are brought to bear in a magical commercial world where companies don't have to make profits and entrepreneurs become gazzillionaires overnight. The new economy with its explosion of entrepreneurial activity mirrors the growth of the internet and information technology. This is no coincidence. The new technology has provided a platform for pent-up entrepreneurial energy.

According to Professor William Sahlman, of Harvard Business School, the new-found entrepreneurial spirit is the bedrock of America's economic renaissance.[49] The new economy is entrepreneur led rather than technology led. Technology is only as good as the uses found for it and the markets identified for its sale. The businesses that emerge as long-term successes from the technology gold rush will be those that are based on business principles of meeting consumer demand rather than those simply based on bright new technology.

virtual visit   **www.thestreet.com**

Says James Cramer, founder of thestreet.com: 'If you want to know who will survive, you need only ask who has more than one potentially profitable revenue stream. If you find a Web business with just one revenue stream, that business will fail. If you find a business that does not include interaction with people at the highest level, that will fail. And if you find a business, and here I have quotation marks around business, that wouldn't look like a business if it were off the Web, don't be fooled. It isn't one. It never will be.'[50] 'Forget about the e-hype,' says Adrian Slywotzky of Mercer Management Consulting. 'Going digital – converting from atoms to bits – gives your company a competitive edge, but only if you focus on the basics: money, talent, customers, and time.'[51]

Indeed, some commentators are warning of the perils of becoming blinded by the bright and insistent light of technology. Often the corporate world's love affair with technology means that technology rather than humanity tends to set the agenda. It is easier to order up a new software package than to discover the tastes and preferences of urban teenagers. Futurist John Naisbitt laments: 'Companies feel pressured into keeping up with technology because they fear falling behind their competitors. They feel they have to be on the internet so move as fast as they can to make the internet their strategy. In effect the promise of the internet is running their businesses.' Not that Naisbitt is a high-tech Luddite: 'I am very much pro-technology, but more discretion is needed.' Naisbitt notes that America finds itself in a zone of technological intoxication – more soberly he judges that 'Europe is generally more appreciative of life's essential pleasures'.[52]

Technological intoxication is characterized by an addiction to quick fixes; the increasing acceptance of violence; confusion as to what is real; and a confused relationship with technology in which fear and worship are combined. The result is that consumer technology and the escape from consumer technology – through holidays, for example – are the two biggest markets in the American economy. Often, however, we seek to escape through buying and using more technology. 'We are tethered to work through mobile phones and the like. We're allowing technology to take over our leisure time,' says Naisbitt.[53]

Whether they are its instigators or merely beneficiaries, gen e are ideally placed to take advantage of the new economy. Central to this is their willingness to view technology as a business tool. Nothing more. Nothing less.

Tools rule. The brightest .com businesses are usually successful because of their ideas and timing rather than their technology. The apparel retailer boo.com is typical of the new breed of success stories. Its founders are in their late twenties – the Swedes Ernst Malmsten and Kajsa Leander. The business was founded in 1998 and a year later had 215 employees (including a cool hunter seeking out the latest trends) and financial backing estimated at around $100 million.

Truth be told, boo.com is hardly rocket science. The big idea is to sell fashionable clothes via the internet. That's it. Now why didn't we think of it? The answer is easy: we are neither cool nor funky. Boo.com is about using technology to tap into the zeitgeist. (And the technology the company uses is not that smart by contemporary standards.) It is about understanding a new breed of fickle, fashion conscious, brand-led consumers. It is about having fingers on the cool pulse.

In this environment where the next big thing is likely to be found on an inner city street, where consumers are addicted to technology, and the ability to connect with reality is paramount, small entrepreneurial companies have a clear advantage. Guys in suits wouldn't have been able to sell boo.com to venture capitalists in a million years. The new economy is an entrepreneurial ferment and it is shaped by entrepreneurs rather than simply by technology.

www.boo.com **virtual visit**

> Gen e are ideally placed to take advantage of the new economy. Central to this is their willingness to view technology as a business tool. Nothing more. Nothing less

> The new economy is an entrepreneurial ferment and it is shaped by entrepreneurs rather than simply by technology

sitting comfortably

T he noisy hype about e-commerce and the internet suggests that ordinary managers need not apply. We are told that the new breed of technological successes are built on inspirational talent rather than upon the management basics. In reality, however, professional management and entrepreneurial essentials are very much to the fore in developing innovative e-commerce ideas. 'The ideas that stand the test of time will, in all likelihood, be those backed by sound management,' says Peter Cohan, author of *Net Profit*.[54]

> Professional management and entrepreneurial essentials are very much to the fore in developing innovative e-commerce ideas

One company which aims to combine the innovative opportunism characteristic of internet businesses and down-to-earth management is Furniture Online, the UK's first **www.furniture-on-line.co.uk** | virtual visit dedicated online furniture store. Throughout its gestation and development, Furniture Online has emphasized traditional fundamentals.

'We take customer service very seriously. People do not purchase furniture frequently and it is a subject most are not entirely comfortable with. Furniture can also represent a large investment and the logistics of delivery can often appear daunting,' says Julian Field, the company's managing director. Field, aged 38, has an MBA from the leading French business school, INSEAD, and spent five years as managing director of Tomlinson Furniture before setting up Furniture Online in May 1999.

To compete effectively, Furniture Online identified the need to cut through the hassle of purchasing furniture and then to deliver the products effectively. Bricks and mortar businesses have largely failed to address either of these issues. As a result, Furniture Online is partly aiming to beat established businesses at their own game. Its delivery service has a personal touch with precise delivery times being agreed in advance with the customer over the telephone. 'There has to be an improvement in the standard of delivery if e-commerce is to really have an effect,' predicts operations director Denzil Vallance.

According to the company's new media director, David Oxley, the company's selling point is not the technology which enables you to visit its website and view sofa-beds and desks in abundance. 'The quality of our service does not depend on how polished our website is but on the commitment of our staff to make shopping for furniture a fun and rewarding experience. We hope our customers will feel that the company is run by people who really care about great furniture.'

Based in Leeds, it took Furniture Online just six months to sign up manufacturers and establish a national home delivery network and a call centre. The speed with which the business was set up is probably its most Silicon Valley-like feature. 'In the summer we were signed up by Yahoo! UK for its new shopping channel. We worked around the clock designing and launching the site and installing customer service systems to meet Yahoo!'s November 1999 deadline,' recalls Julian Field. Furniture Online was launched with 40 suppliers and around 150 products. The aim is to have over 200 suppliers and 10,000 products.

Unlike in other e-commerce businesses, Julian Field plays down talk of eliminating traditional retail stores. Bricks and clicks will survive fruitfully together. Although he expects many consumers to continue to buy furniture in the traditional way, he predicts that the market for online furniture will grow steadily as people become more comfortable shopping over the internet. 'The UK domestic furniture market is currently worth £7.3 billion per annum in retail sales. We anticipate that as the internet market matures in the UK, we could see online sales accounting for up to 15 per cent of the total furniture market. Shopping for furniture in the high street has many drawbacks which shopping online overcomes,' he says. 'You would have to spend many hours in a car on a weekend visiting showrooms to view a range of furniture as broad as ours with no guarantee of finding what you are looking for.'

Closer to home, one of the problems encountered by Furniture Online is that internet users still tend to be predominantly male while women play the leading role in furniture purchasing. Julian Field remains suspicious of the obvious solution to this – costly advertising and promotion in women's magazines and newspapers. 'You can raise a lot of money from venture capitalists and then spend it on full page ads in national newspapers. But how many clicks does it take to make a sale?' Field would like to know. He didn't attend business school for nothing and is eager to seize and utilize the data gathered from people visiting the company's website.

> 'We've proved that e-commerce is not some ethereal concept, but one which reliably delivers products to people's doors at competitive prices. There's nothing mysterious in that'

As well as emphasizing service and delivery, Furniture Online is financially cautious. Profits are anticipated after three years. The company was launched without recourse to venture capitalists. But having launched and become first to market in the UK, the company is developing a business plan to attract venture capital. Says Julian Field: 'This is a business which works, built on a proven idea, and with management structures and values already in place. We've proved that e-commerce is not some ethereal concept, but one which reliably delivers products to people's doors at competitive prices. There's nothing mysterious in that.'

the new economy is here to stay

O f course, not everyone buys this. In spite of James Dyson's sound advice, a lot of people still wear suits. The Fortune 500 still wield some power. Some see the new economy as a mirage – a caffeine-induced hallucination; little more than a speculative bubble. This is wishful thinking on their part. Responding to recent concerns that the .com bubble might burst, Harvard's William Sahlman is bullish. Concerns about the 'irrational exuberance' of the capital markets and inflation, raised by the Federal Reserve, are unfounded, he says. The only danger is from government interference. 'Chicken Little told us that the sky was falling. Alan Greenspan and his cohorts at the Fed believe it just might … I'm here to assure you that Chicken Little and Alan Greenspan have a lot in common; they fret for no good reason,' says Sahlman.

The reality, he says, is that the sky – that is, the US economy – is just fine, thank you. In fact, it's never been better. And it will stay that way for many years to come if the government just manages to stay out of its way. The new economy, in Sahlman's view, is strong for four very good reasons. First, it is based on a business model that works – one that continually ratchets up efficiency. The old American economy was characterized by bloated companies protected by carefully constructed entry barriers, which was fine until the 1970s when foreign competitors descended on the party like locusts. The results were large-scale redundancies and a great deal of perplexed head scratching. The tough times of the 1970s, though, planted the seeds for the entrepreneurship of today, says Sahlman. The new model was invented by people like Bill Gates and Michael Dell – and is being continuously reinvented by new arrivals. Its great virtue is that it encourages efficiency. 'Any model that relentlessly drives out inefficiencies, forces intelligent business process reengineering and gives customers more of what they want is bound to be sustainable,' Sahlman contends.

> An army of entrepreneurs is on the march. Armed only with their laptops, bright ideas for .com start-ups and a fistful of domain names, they are generation e

Second, although economists normally don't give much credence to it, the new economy is built on America's admiration for entrepreneurs and its tolerance for failure. These factors give rise to easy access to capital.

The third reason why the new economy is strong, to Sahlman's mind, is that it is attracting the 'best and brightest minds in the country'.

Finally, the new economy is strong because, although initially an American phenomenon, it is now spreading around the world. From Palo Alto, California, to Bangalore, India, from Boston to Beijing, an army of entrepreneurs is on the march. Armed only with their laptops, bright ideas for .com start-ups and a fistful of domain names, they are generation e. Revolution is in the air – and is likely to stay there.

the Dell model

f there is one person who inspires gen e above all others, that person is Michael Dell. He is the role model, the exemplar of what can be done. Michael Dell is proof that the new economy is not a mirage, but commercial reality. Dell made history when he became the youngest CEO ever to run a Fortune 500 company. Today he heads one of the most profitable and innovative businesses in the world. Along the way, he has joined the ranks of the most revered entrepreneurs in the USA – as the man who took the direct sales model and elevated it to an art form. (In 1999, Dell Computer came fourth in Fortune's ranking of America's Most Admired Companies, behind GE, Coca-Cola and Microsoft.)

> If there is one person who inspires gen e above all others, that person is Michael Dell. He is the role model, the exemplar of what can be done

The company Dell built is not the biggest in the world. Nor are its products the most innovative. Dell Corporation is that rarity: a corporate model, the benchmark for how companies can be organized and managed to reap the full potential of technology. Michael Dell is the Alfred P. Sloan of the high-tech age. But while it took Sloan decades to meld General Motors into his organizational image, Michael Dell is still a young man – a mere 35.

Dell started young. By the age of 13, he had become a dab hand at taking apart the motherboard of his Apple II computer. But his interest in business pre-dated even that. 'I first experienced the power – and rewards – of being direct when I was 12 years old,' Dell says. 'The father of my best friend in Houston was a pretty avid stamp collector, so naturally my friend and I wanted to get into stamp collecting, too … I started reading stamp journals just for fun, and soon began noticing that stamp prices were rising. Before long, my interest in stamps began to shift from the joy of collecting to the idea that there was something here that my mother, a stockbroker, would have termed a "commercial opportunity".'

Dinnertime conversations in the Dell household reinforced his interest. The talk was about what the Federal Reserve was doing and how it affected the American economy; the oil crisis; and which company stocks to buy and sell. By the age of 16, young Michael was putting what he'd learned into practice.

He got a summer job selling newspaper subscriptions of the *Houston Post* and quickly realized that the list of phone numbers the company handed out was an inefficient way to drum up new business. Dell speedily identified a pattern for new subscribers. Feedback from potential customers convinced him that the best groups to target were newlyweds and people who had just bought new houses or apartments.

From the local courthouse he and his friends obtained lists of those who had applied for marriage licences. From another source he compiled a list of people who had recently applied for mortgages. He targeted the two groups with a personalized letter. Subscriptions poured in.

When the school term started, an assignment from his history and economics teacher asked students to complete a tax return. Dell calculated his income based on his successful newspaper subscriptions business at $18,000. His teacher, assuming he had put the decimal point in the wrong place, corrected it. She was dismayed to learn that there was no mistake – her student had made more money than she had.

By then the fledgling entrepreneur had a new hobby – computers. While at the University of Texas, he rebuilt PCs and sold them. His business was kick-started with a $1,000 investment. Dell is living proof that having too little capital is better than too much. It forced him to reinvent the computer industry. Dell's 16 per cent share of the company is now worth some $5 billion.

Dell's inspiration was to realize that PCs could be built to order and sold directly to customers. This had two clear advantages. First, it meant that the company was not hostage to retailers intent on increasing their mark-ups at its expense. Dell cut out the middlemen. By doing so, he reduced the company's selling costs from a typical 12 per cent of revenue to a mere 4 to 6 per cent.

Second, the company did not need to carry large stocks. It actually carries around eleven days of inventory. 'The best indirect company has 38 days on inventory. The average channel has about 45 days of inventory. So if you put it together, you've got 80 days or so of inventory – a little less than eight times our inventory level,' says Michael Dell.

> In any language, high profit margins and low costs make business sense. In the fast-growing computer business they are nirvana

In any language, high profit margins and low costs make business sense. In the fast-growing computer business they are nirvana. In its first eight years Dell grew at a steady rate of 80 per cent. It then slowed down to a positively snail-like 55 per cent. Its 1998 revenues were $12.3 billion.

Little wonder, perhaps, that Dell's competitors look pedestrian in comparison. While Dell has been growing explosively, Compaq has been growing at less than 20 per cent. (Dell has now overtaken Compaq.) Inspired by such raw statistics emulators have come thick and fast. Emulation is the purest form of desperation as well as flattery. Dell's insight was, after all, blissfully simple. 'There is a popular idea now that if you reduce your inventory and build to order, you'll be just like Dell. Well, that's one part of the puzzle, but there are other parts, too,' Dell has said. He explains the company's success as 'a disciplined approach to under-standing how we create value in the PC industry, selecting the right markets, staying focused on a clear business model and just executing'.

While the notion of selling direct is appealing, companies which do so are only as good as their ability to deliver. Dell's model creates a direct line to the customer which the company has proved highly adept at maximizing. Direct knowledge of the end consumer builds a satisfied customer base – increasing Dell's brand strength, lowering customer acquisition costs and boosting customer loyalty. The result is 'mass customization' as opposed to the traditional method of broad market segmentation.

Dell, the interloper which has cut out the money-grabbing middleman, has a strong rapport with its customers – in a way that Microsoft, for example, has manifestly failed to achieve. 'To all our nit-picky – over-demanding – ask awkward questions customers. Thank you, and keep up the good work,' read one Dell advertisement. 'You actually get to have a relationship with the customer,' explains Michael Dell. 'And that creates valuable information, which in turn allows us to leverage our relationships with both suppliers and customers. Couple that information with technology and you have the infrastructure to revolutionize the fundamental business models of major global companies.'

Dell has proved highly efficient in utilizing the full power of modern technology to create reliable logistic and distribution systems. It is among the pioneers of selling by the internet. 'The internet for us is a dream come true,' says Dell. 'It's like zero-variable-cost transaction. The only thing better would be mental telepathy.' Dell's online sales alone exceed $3 million a day and, during Christmas 1997, Dell was selling $6 million worth of products every day online. The company's web site is expected to transact half of Dell's transactions by the year 2000.

virtual visit   **www.dell.com**

The beauty of the Dell model is that it can be applied to a range of industries where middlemen have creamed off profits. Its low overheads also mean that Michael Dell has no need to mortgage the business to expand. This year's model may be around for some time. The same can be said of the man who built it.

With the company's stock up 36,000 per cent over the last ten years, Dell has grown from a $159 million company to an $18 billion colossus. With that sort of performance, many a CEO would be pleased to take a bow and enjoy the applause. Michael Dell merely describes it as a 'great start'. 'I believe we have the right business model for the internet age. We have a significant lead in dealing direct with customers and suppliers,' he notes.

If that's a good start, what's he going to do for an encore? At 34, remember, he's still just a slip of a lad – a whole decade younger than Bill Gates. When people ask whether the growth will slow down, he points out that his company happens to be part of what could soon be the largest industry in the world and, just for good measure, adds that the company still has only 9 per cent of total market share.

'If we had 50 per cent market share – like Coca-Cola – I might be a little more concerned about our growth slowing,' says Dell. 'There's no such thing as a company that executes perfectly forever. But the real key to our success comes from within … It comes from being willing to challenge conventional wisdom and having the courage to follow our convictions. It comes from an innate fascination with eliminating unnecessary steps.' Unnecessary steps beware – you have been warned.

beyond Silicon Valley

Gen e have a natural affinity with technology and are drawn to the high-tech clusters that now dot the world. They use it to seek out kindred spirits. The best known hotspot is California's Silicon Valley – although it has now been joined by other high concentrations of gen e activity. Silicon Valley companies are now valued at four times those of Detroit; and their value almost equals that of the entire French stock market. Palo Alto, California, is now home to 7,000 electronics and software firms. While major cities around the world routinely fight to stage the next Olympic games, Palo Alto seemed to host the entire technological revolution. Every movement needs its spiritual home. Palo Alto is gen e's.

> Gen e have a natural affinity with technology and are drawn to the high-tech clusters that now dot the world. They use it to seek out kindred spirits

This fact and the burgeoning confidence of Silicon Valley are routinely celebrated. When asked if he thought IBM had a chance of leading the next stage of the information revolution, Gary Hamel (co-author of the influential best seller *Competing for the Future*) replied: 'I'd need to know how many of IBM's top 100 executives had grown up on the west coast of America where the future of the computer industry is being created and how many were under forty years of age. If a quarter or a

> Every movement needs its spiritual home. Palo Alto is gen e's

third of the senior group were both under forty and possessed a west coast perspective, IBM has a chance.'[55]

Hamel recounts that in 1998 Silicon Valley companies produced 41 IPOs. By January 1999 these had a total market capitalization of some $27 billion. This means that these companies generated $54,000 in new wealth per worker in one year. (Extrapolating these figures, Hamel points out that with its 594,000 employees, General Motors should be looking at generating $32 billion worth of new wealth.) Then comes the $64,000 question: 'Did your business create that much new wealth last year?'

Probably not. Hamel is dismissive of the old business establishment. (He is not the only one.) Traditional companies spend their time deciding where their resources would be most effectively utilized rather than investing time in attracting the right resources, he suggests. They are more interested in stewardship than entrepreneurship – 'Stewards polish grandma's silver – they buff up the assets and capabilities they inherited from entrepreneurs long retired or long dead.'

We stand at the threshold of the new business world. Silicon Valley is a symbol of what Hamel calls the innovation frontier. 'We are at the dawn of a new industrial order. We are leaving behind a world in which scale, efficiency and replication were everything. We are taking our first few tentative steps into a world where imagination, experimentation, and agility are, if not everything, at least the essential catalysts for wealth creation,' he says.

Herein lies the difference between the business model of Silicon Valley and that pursued by mere mortals. 'The Valley is the distilled essence of entrepreneurial energy,' says Hamel, with typical colour and no little hyperbole. In Silicon Valley, ideas, talent and capital move in perpetual freeflow. They move where the money can be made – or will be made at some time in the future. In traditional companies, ideas, talent and capital ossify rather than multiply.

Hamel's solution? Companies may not be in Silicon Valley, but often they possess the capital, the market know-how, the logistics and the human talent to behave along the lines of the Silicon Valley model. Entrepreneurial behaviour does not acknowledge neat geographical divisions. 'Many corporate leaders envy the success of Silicon Valley's entrepreneurs, but few have thought about how they might bring the Valley inside – how they might ignite the entrepreneurial passions of their own people,' Hamel laments. 'They assume the Valley is filled with brilliant visionaries while their own organizations are filled with witless drones.'

It is not that traditional companies cannot, but they choose not to. In doing so, they are choosing to be poor rather than to dedicate themselves and their resources to wealth creation. The choice, says Hamel, is theirs.

Gary Hamel is always entertaining and usually right. But in this case we have to disagree with some of his conclusions. Indeed, one problem we have with all the coverage and hyperbole surrounding the new economy is that it is far too often interpreted as something restricted to the USA. This is as unfortunate as it is inaccurate. The West Coast does not have a monopoly of anything – though it has a lot of oranges. People are innovative, imaginative and entrepreneurial throughout the world. Gen e are inhabitants of planet Earth.

> People are innovative, imaginative and entrepreneurial throughout the world. Gen e are inhabitants of planet Earth

The concentration on Silicon Valley actually serves to mask some problems in the American economy. It is hugely successful but, despite what you may have read, it is far from perfect – no economy can be. The USA is not the economic nirvana which it is often portrayed as.

In his book, *In Praise of Hard Industries*, Eamonn Fingleton[56] cites evidence that 20 per cent of the American workforce could be marginalized by the move to an information-based economy. He also argues that the new economy has failed to provide income growth for Americans. In terms of per capita income, the USA lags behind eight countries. What distinguishes these countries, says Fingleton, is their commitment to manufacturing. (The exceptions are the tax haven of Luxembourg and oil-rich Norway.)

Among the countries outperforming the USA in income terms are Japan and Germany. Both possess a strong manufacturing tradition, undimmed by the dramas of the last decade. 'The impression that the Japanese economy "collapsed" in the 1990s is a myth,' writes Fingleton, pointing to strong income growth as evidence of Japanese robustness. Japanese workers enjoy an average hourly wage of $21.01; German workers receive $14.79; and Americans $12.37. The USA, it seems, is the low-wage economy.

While the USA has embraced every technological advancement with enthusiasm, Japan and Germany have patently lagged behind. This, Fingleton suggests, is likely to be proved a smart strategy. American productivity has not shot though the roof as a result of massive investments in the latest technology. Indeed, productivity increases remain stubbornly low. As Nobel economist Robert Solow put it: 'You can see the computer age everywhere but in the productivity statistics.'

Eamonn Fingleton's final case against the new economy is that it fails to provide much-needed exports. Cultural differences, international regulation and inadequate legal protection for things such as intellectual property rights undermine the export potential of new economy industries.

The message is that although the USA may like to think it has conquered the world, the world is ready to strike back. The USA does not have a monopoly on creativity. Witness the burgeoning Indian software development industry and the fact that there are estimated to be in excess of 100,000 foreign-born engineers in Silicon Valley. Claiming that innate American creativity offers some sort of competitive advantage is, therefore, dangerous ground.

The fact that many of the important breakthroughs have occurred outside the fabled valley seems to have conveniently skipped the collective memory of those who live and work there. Most notably, Microsoft, based in Redmond, Washington. What successful outsiders have done is what gen e does: create their own clusters of expertise. (The success of Silicon Valley also highlights a paradox. Technology was supposed to make it possible to work from anywhere in the world. But in the technology business, face-to-face contact still matters. This is counter-intuitive: despite the spread of technology that enables people to work remotely, location matters more and more.)

Co-founder of Sun Microsystems Bill Joy, another key figure in the gen e story, also turned his back on the enchanted valley. While still a student, Joy shaped

AT&T's Unix operating system, the main competitor to Microsoft's Windows. He's also credited with designing the most crucial circuits in Sun's SPARC microprocessor, which drives the company's workstations and servers. At the end of the 1980s, he moved to Aspen, Colorado. Received Silicon Valley wisdom was that by moving his small research team away from the action, he would lose touch with the decision makers and the buzz in the valley. But the change of scene gave him the opportunity to focus on the language he thought could be the future of the internet. A project called Oak had been developed to support interactive TV, which hadn't materialized. It was ahead of its time, but he could see its potential. In Aspen, it was transformed into Java. The rest, as they say, is history.

Such stories slide by unnoticed in California. Silicon Valley was the right place at the right time. The myth endures. But others are catching on. The next Silicon Valley could, it must be said, be virtually anywhere on earth. After all, in the Far East there is Silicon Island in Taiwan. There is Silicon Plateau in Bangalore (a city with 150,000 software programmers). Then there is the cringingly entitled Softopia in Gifu, Japan; and Media Valley now being developed in Inchon, Korea. Spotting the place to be has never been harder. The top tip seems to be to relocate to a place with the word silicon in its name. (There are plenty to choose from.)

Bill Gates's view of history in the post-industrial era is instructive. 'Which countries and companies are best prepared to take advantage of the information age that is revolutionizing society? When you think about it, 15 years ago this country almost had an inferiority complex about its ability to compete in the world,' he says. 'Everybody was talking about how the Japanese had taken over consumer electronics and [saying] that the computer industry was going to be next, and that their system of hard work somehow was superior, and that we had to completely rethink what we were doing. Now, if you look at what's happened in personal computers or in business in general, or at how we allocate capital, and how we let labor move around, the US has emerged in a very strong position. And so the first beneficiary of all this information technology has been the US.'

In Gates's view, Silicon Valley was in the first phase of the revolution, but that doesn't mean its place is guaranteed in the second phase. 'In places like Singapore, Hong Kong, and the Scandinavian countries,' he notes, 'people are adopting the technology at basically the same rate that we are. And there are a few countries that, relative to their level of income, are going after the technology at an even higher rate than we are because they believe so much in education. In Korea and in many parts of China we see incredible penetration of personal computers even at very low income levels, because people there have decided it's a tool to help their kids get ahead.'

'The whole world is going to benefit in a big way. There will be this shift where, instead of your income level being determined by what country you are from, it will be determined by your education level. Today, a PhD in India doesn't make nearly as much as a PhD in the US. When we get the internet allowing services and advice to be transported as efficiently as goods are transported via shipping, then you'll get essentially open-market bidding for that engineer in India vs. an engineer here in the US. And that benefits everyone, because you're taking better advantage of those resources. So the developed countries will get the early benefit of these things. But in the long run, the people in developing countries who are lucky enough to get a good education should get absolutely the biggest boost from all this.' Education not location is the key.

Education not location is the key

e hotbeds

arvard Business School's Michael Porter is one of the titans of business thinking. His five forces framework, developed in the 1980 bestseller *Competitive Strategy*, is one of the most popular – and plagiarized – business models in history.[57] While the merits, or otherwise, of the five forces continue to be debated and taught, Porter has moved studiously on. His work is notable for its academic rigour and weighty tone. He is no populist and takes on some of the received orthodoxies of globalization.

Theory suggests that the globalization of markets, rapid transportation and high-speed communications capability should allow companies to source anything from anywhere, any time. But, argues Porter, the reality is very different.

The global theory fails to explain the remarkably high success rate of firms specializing in the same disciplines operating in close geographical proximity. Porter points to clusters, critical masses of linked industries and institutions in a particular place that enjoy unusual competitive success in a particular field. The most famous examples, he says, are computer firms in Silicon Valley and the Hollywood film industry, but other such clusters are dotted around the globe.

The proximity of organizations within these clusters – including suppliers, academic institutions and government agencies – appears to affect competition in three broad ways. First, proximity increases the productivity of companies in the region. Second, it drives the direction and pace of innovation. Third, it stimulates and triggers the genesis of new businesses within the cluster.

According to Porter, this phenomenon is probably best explained by the notion of a closer knit community; one where geographical, cultural and institutional closeness confers on insiders special access to each other's skills and ideas.

> Gen e buy Porter's theory. They cluster with abandon.

Gen e buy Porter's theory. They cluster with abandon. Whether it is the Formula One cluster in southern England or the textile/apparel cluster in northern Italy, gen e gather together in hotbeds of enterprise. Emergent locations include: Oulu, Finland; Cambridge, England; Stockholm, Sweden; Sophia Antipolis, France; Karlsruhe, Germany; Tel Aviv, Israel; Hsinchu, Taiwan.

Oulu, Finland

If you're talking high tech, Finland is the place to be. It is home to Nokia, maker of the sexiest and most stylish mobiles phones on the market. It is, admittedly, a lot colder than California (-20°C in December), but Finland has cast off its traditional business image. It now exports more electronics than forestry products. The Finns also have more internet hosts per capita than any other country. The star performing region in Finland

> If you're talking high tech, Finland is the place to be

is Oulu. Oulu's population has trebled to 110,000 since its technology university was set up in 1959. This is Europe's northernmost concentration of industry and know-how – of that there is no doubt. On the edge of the Arctic, Oulu boasts Oulu Technopolis, a purpose-built technology park already home to 150 companies and set to be floated on the stock market.

Cambridge, England

Admittedly Cambridge has been popular for some time. But now it is blessed with the close by but dreadfully named Silicon Fen (an offspring of the Scottish Silicon

Glen where *Braveheart* meets Bill Gates). Silicon Fen has been celebrated by, among others, the *New York Times*, which noted with its customary accuracy: 'This is no Silicon Valley. The pace here is neither frenetic nor flashy, and people frown on loud manifestations of wealth.' The Cambridge area has a strong technological pedigree. It was home to one of the UK's first science parks and Fen converts include Olivetti Research Laboratories and Acorn Computer Group. The biggest deal, of course, was the $80 million Microsoft facility. Big bucks. All Cambridge needs is for a movie with Hugh Grant to be filmed nearby and it would hit the Palo Alto style bonanza.

> All Cambridge needs is for a movie with Hugh Grant to be filmed nearby and it would hit the Palo Alto style bonanza

Stockholm, Sweden

Two of the fastest growing web design companies are Swedish – Icon Medialab and Spray/Razorfish. The home of Abba can even boast that it is the third largest music exporter in the world. Happening? You'd better believe it. If you want to find the high-tech hub of Stockholm try the suburb of Kista. Helpfully it is often now called Kiselsta – not coincidentally, 'kisel' is the Swedish for silicon, but don't allow that to put you off.

> The home of Abba can even boast that it is the third largest music exporter in the world. Happening? You'd better believe it

Then there are its up and coming business gurus, Kjell Nordström and Jonas Ridderstråle. 'IT increasingly makes location irrelevant. You can be anywhere,' says Ridderstråle. 'On the other hand, IT and face-to-face contact seem to have much the same relationship as paper and the paperless office. The more we use IT, the more we need to travel. Perhaps the future will demand more nomadic people.'

Sophia Antipolis, France

Warmth and high tech. Sophia Antipolis is Palo Alto with better food. It is home to the largest European scientific park (and there are now 300 such parks in

Europe), just 15 minutes from Nice airport. It has also been rated by one US magazine as one of the 'top ten hottest tech cities in the world'. Sophia Antipolis is home to, among others, the Theseus Institute. Sophia Antipolis has been a slow-burning project. For 15 years it has made steady progress without grabbing the imagination. Perhaps now its time has come.

> Warmth and high tech. Sophia Antipolis is Palo Alto with better food

Karlsruhe, Germany

Karlsruhe is being aggressively pushed as an alternative to the major German business cities. (And among German cities, big companies are looking east towards Dresden and the Elbe Valley.) In Karlsruhe a new technology park is focusing marketing minds wonderfully. The town's statistics are impressive. One ranking of comparative economic power put Karlsruhe as sixth in Germany behind Stuttgart, Frankfurt, Munich, Düsseldorf and Köln, but ahead of Berlin. At the same time, Karlsruhe's strength is that it isn't a big city – its population is only 270,000. The town boasts the Centre for Art and Media Technology, a European school, Baden cuisine and, crucially, the most sunshine days in Germany. More seriously, Bosch, Siemens, Daimler-Benz and Michelin have a presence in the town.

> Bosch, Siemens, Daimler-Benz and Michelin have a presence in the town

Tel Aviv, Israel

In the early 1990s, Israel was not exactly renowned for its high-tech capabilities – despite having a highly educated workforce and few natural resources. Then the Israeli government decided to pump money into supporting the country's entrepreneurs. Its venture capital provided a kick-start. Before long money was pouring into high-tech start-ups from inside and outside the country – minimal investment had mushroomed to over $500 million by 1998. The result is Silicon Wadi – wadi, as

> The result is Silicon Wadi – wadi, as you will have guessed, means valley

you will have guessed, means valley. The heart of the Wadi is Tel Aviv where 85 high-tech companies are based at Atidim Park alone.

Hsinchu, Taiwan

Professor Chong Ju Choi, director of the MBA program at the Judge Institute of Management at Cambridge University and an authority on globalization, points to Taiwan as a prime example of the centres of excellence in emerging economies. The Hsinchu Science-Based Industrial Park, established in 1981, is the centre for Taiwan's high-tech electronics and information industries. The Park is noted for its innovative research and development projects. It was created

> 'Hsinchu is worth one-third of Silicon Valley in terms of revenues and profits'

with funding from an enlightened Taiwanese government (from 1980 to 1995 it allocated $483 million to it). 'Today,' says Professor Choi, 'Hsinchu is worth one-third of Silicon Valley in terms of revenues and profits. Talk to people in Silicon Valley and you realize that the American high-tech companies have been outsourcing on a large scale for 20 years.'

So successful has Hsinchu been that the Taiwanese government is now developing a second science and technology centre. Elsewhere, others are coming up fast, including the so-called Silicon Fen science and technology park based around Cambridge University, where Professor Choi is now based.

'The emerging economies provide outstanding sources of skills and expertise,' says Professor Choi, 'but there are two key points to recognize. The first is that technology is the great equalizer. As the COBOL example shows, it makes a worker in India as productive as one in North America or Western Europe. The person in India may have a better education and better technology than someone in London or Paris. But people in the developed economies tend to assume that the technology and skills in emerging economies lag behind. Ten years ago this would probably have been true, but not any longer. Many of the emerging countries have not had to work through the old technology. Take the example of mobile phones where the digital technology replaced the old analogue exchanges – many emerging economies will skip analogue altogether and go straight to digital.'

The second point, according to Professor Choi, is that globalization requires new ways of looking at the world. 'In the past, people assumed that the world was divided geographically, so it was split into North America, Europe and Asia. But what we're actually seeing now is that it can be divided into mature economies and emerging economies. It's like cutting the world up in a different way.

'Why did the fall-out from Russia affect Brazil? It shows the economic linkage between these countries. The trouble is that global or international companies don't have much experience in managing this. Traditionally, they have tried to source skills for Asian markets in Asia. But experience in an emerging economy is relevant to any other emerging economy. A manager who has worked in Poland will understand the issues not just in Poland and Hungary, but in Brazil or Indonesia. This affects the whole personnel and recruitment side of the business.'

power shifts

brawn to brain

Gen e are also a catalyst for wider changes in the world. They are involved in and identified with major power shifts – political, social and economic. The overall changes are to an economy and society which are driven by intellects and information, rather than by brawn and one-dimensional thinking.

In *Funky Business*, Kjell Nordström and Jonas Ridderstråle note: 'In an information desert, companies rule. But now we are re-entering an information jungle where information is again available at our fingertips. We are back in the bazaar – though this time it resides in cyberspace, the net neighborhood.'[58] This bazaar is home to gen e.

> 'We are back in the bazaar – though this time it resides in cyberspace, the net neighborhood.' This bazaar is home to gen e

The information age places a premium on intellectual work. There is growing realization that recruiting, retaining and nurturing talented people are crucial to competitiveness. Intellectual capital is the height of corporate fashion. The challenge is that talent or intellectual capital is a scarce and, therefore, highly prized resource. (This is one, but by no means the only, explanation for booming executive pay.)

> Intellectual capital is the height of corporate fashion.

The rise in interest is understandable and, perhaps, woefully late in the evolution of industrial life. 'Of course, knowledge has always mattered, but two things have changed,' argues Thomas Stewart, author of *Intellectual Capital*. 'First, as a percentage of the value added to a product it has grown to be the most important thing. Costs used to be 80 per cent on material and 20 per cent on knowledge – now it is split 70–30 the other way. Second, it is increasingly possible to manage knowledge.'[59]

Managing ideas, imagination and know-how, however, has so far proved elusive. Knowledge workers – software developers, advertising executives and other creative souls, who can turn it on and off at the tap – are worth their weight in gold.

> Knowledge workers – software developers, advertising executives and other creative souls, who can turn it on and off at the tap – are worth their weight in gold

The bust-up at the former advertising agency Saatchi and Saatchi, which led to the departure of Maurice Saatchi and his coterie at the end of 1994, Stewart argues, wiped out a proportion of the company's intellectual capital. As a result, it lost key client accounts and the share price fell. The new knowledge economy, says Stewart, also augurs the 'end of management as we know it'. 'The rise of the knowledge worker fundamentally alters the nature of work and the agenda of management. Managers are custodians; they protect and care for the assets of a corporation; when the assets are intellectual, the manager's job changes.'

> The logic of the management pyramid – a small number of people telling a large number of others what to do – is redundant

In essence, Stewart's argument is that the rise of knowledge workers means that the bosses no longer know more than the workers (if they ever really did). As a result, the logic of the management pyramid – a small number of people telling a large number of others what to do – is redundant.

Much of the traditional role of managers is based on Taylorism – after Frederick Taylor, the industrial engineer who founded scientific management at the turn of the twentieth century. In his own way Taylor, who was famed for time and motion studies in factories, was a knowledge worker. He used his stopwatch to break down complex processes into simple tasks, thereby increasing efficiency.

However, Taylor saw the way that management organized labour as the limit of intellectual capital. In effect, he saw workers as nothing more than the components in a machine which was operated by management. Today's knowledge workers, however, are much more than simply cogs and wheels. What has changed is that the value these workers add comes not from the machines they operate but from the application of what they know.

Gen e carry the tools of their trade with them between their ears. It is they and not their managers who are the experts and must decide how best to deploy their know-how. As a result, what they do has more in common with work carried out by people in the professions and must be assessed not by the tasks performed but by the results achieved.

> Gen e carry the tools of their trade with them between their ears

'A lawyer is not evaluated on the number of words in her closing argument but on how well chosen and effective they are; not on the number of footnotes in her brief but on whether it makes a winning argument,' Stewart says. The lawyer doesn't have a boss telling her how to do her job: she has a client, a customer, who expects her to plan and organize her own work – but, he might add, is totally unqualified to tell her how to do it.

From this, he says, it follows that the professional model of organizational design should supersede the bureaucratic. So where does this leave managers? The answer, Stewart suggests, is that the only legitimate role for managers is around the task of leadership – although they don't yet have a proper understanding of what's involved. He says: 'If "values" and "vision" and "empowerment" and "teamwork" and "facilitating" and "coaching" sometimes sound like so much mush-mouthed mish-mash – which they sometimes are – that's a reflection of the fact that managers are groping towards a language and a means for managing knowledge, knowledge work, and knowledge intensive companies.'

'Intelligence becomes an asset when some useful order is created out of free-floating brainpower,' says Stewart. In other words, organizational intellect becomes intellectual capital only 'when it can be deployed to do something that could not be done if it remained scattered around like so many coins in a gutter'.

Intellectual capital is useful knowledge that is packaged for others. In this way, a mailing list, a database or a process can be turned into intellectual capital if someone inside the organization decides to 'describe, share and exploit what's unique and powerful about the way the company operates'.

Intellectual capital is useful knowledge that is packaged for others

The trouble is that many of those who own the knowledge are no longer prepared to share it with what they perceive as greedy corporations.

thinkers for the new age

The shift from brawn to brain brings a new generation of thinkers. While management gurus are among the most powerful opinion formers of our age, the days of some of the well-established gurus appear numbered. They have been left behind by tumultuous technological change. All the talk of e-commerce, the internet and the miracles of technology has left some great thinkers strapped to the starting blocks. They are out of tune with gen e.

> The shift from brawn to brain brings a new generation of thinkers

For example, established gurus such as Rosabeth Moss Kanter, Charles Handy and Michael Porter have minimal and uninspiring presences on the internet. In addition, those weaned on a diet of big corporate names find it difficult to look elsewhere for best management practice. Their work often recites the usual suspects as corporate exemplars rather than seeking out new and original material. If you are used to talking about General Motors, Spray/Razorfish may be difficult to come to terms with.

> The new group of gurus – labelled *guritos* – is technology friendly

The new generation of gurus – labelled *guritos* – is technology friendly. They are as likely to establish their website before their book is published or research undertaken. Indeed, the website can be a research tool. Their audience is managers who see being up to date with technology as vital.

Alistair Owens, marketing director of Economatics, the Sheffield-based distributor of engineering supplies, is a voracious business book reader. 'An effective management guru is a prophet. Assuming there is no divine intervention, he has the duty to research, develop and test theories in as wide a theatre of operation as possible,' says Owens. 'A modern guru who is not using the internet in their research is akin to the man who thought that electricity was there to help light the gas lamp.'

Somewhat surprisingly, one of the exceptions to this process of renewal in the guru business is one of the biggest gurus of them all, Tom Peters. Peters was co-author of *In Search of Excellence,* whose publication in 1982 effectively ignited the business book and guru industries. He has embraced the internet with charac-teristic enthusiasm. Indeed, Peters has used the internet to revitalize his standing in the guru marketplace.

With declining book sales – largely inevitable after his first book sold over six million copies – Peters appeared to be heading nowhere fast. The arrival of the internet changed things. While other gurus base their work on ornately constructed research, Peters is a magpie, gathering nuggets of information, examples and inspiration from a profusion of sources. The internet suits Tom Peters.

Peters argues that the onus should be on branding yourself. We are all brands now. He has attempted to practise what he preaches by rebranding his business.

virtual visit **www.tompeters.com**

During 1999, www.tompeters.com was launched. The guru has found the move into the internet a sometimes salutary experience. 'I made mistake after mistake. Sub-contracting the website didn't work – ironic as I am a champion of sub-contracting. Our plans were too grand, too quick and kept falling apart,' says Peters. He now professes greater understanding while remaining as mystified as anyone as to how to make money from the internet. 'Web sites are living entities. It is a playful medium, one where if you change your mind you can erase it,' he says.

Peters' willingness to move with the times has reaped dividends. He is back towards the front of the guru pack – 'This is the age of constant hype so you have to find ways to stoke the fire. I don't know anyone else who does what I do who is up there' – and continues a relentless schedule of seminar appearances criss-crossing the globe.

'There is always an immediate sense of redundancy in many management gurus' ideas. They are after all purveyors of management fashions,' says guru watcher Timothy Clark of King's College, University of London. 'Many gurus cannot repeat the success of their first book and so have no staying power. Where Peters differs is in his gift of sensing the importance of trends in management at a very early stage. I am sure that this is one reason why he gives so many talks. He can get a feel of what is going on and at the same time test his ideas on his key audience – managers. His use and advocacy of the internet is just the latest example.'[60]

> On a brightly lit stage is a tall figure dressed in black. His head is shaved. Bangles jangle around his wrist

The reality is that each new generation is led by its own breed of gurus. Think of the average management guru. Male and American. Probably a professor from a big name business school, wearing an unobtrusive suit. He has, in all likelihood, little on-stage presence but a brain the size of a small country.

Think again. The emergent gen e gurus are not like that at all. On a brightly lit stage is a tall figure dressed in black. His head is shaved. Bangles jangle around his wrist. He is talking about the embalming of Lenin, the Pope making a CD and the niche marketing of a magazine called *Legshow*. His subject is management but not management as we know it. Welcome to the funky world of Kjell Nordström and Jonas Ridderstråle.

The Swedes Nordström and Ridderstråle are gurus with a difference, rising stars in a market traditionally dominated by Americans. The only similarity between the Swedish duo and conventional gurus is their jobs – they are academics at the Stockholm School of Economics. (Nordström is also involved with a variety of decidedly funky companies including the Norwegian firm Stokke Fabrikker, Swedish internet company Spray Ventures, and the US digital change agent Razorfish.) Their gigs – not seminars – are packed out whenever they appear in Scandinavia and increasingly beyond. The launch of their book, *Funky Business*, marks Nordström and Ridderstråle's promotion to the major guru league.

Their message is uncompromisingly challenging. People do not attend their gigs in search of a pat on the back and reassurance about what a great job they're doing. And, if they do, they are likely to be disappointed. A typical gig opens with the observation: 'Karl Marx was right.' The audience shuffle, revelling in their discomfort as only business people are capable of doing, as the duo launch into a powerful critique of new business realities. This is not what the audience learned at Harvard Business School.

When it comes to gen e they are defiantly and definitely on message. Their message is, they say, revolutionary and it is difficult to preach business revolution if you wear the uniform of the regime being overthrown. 'Changes in technology, our institutions and our values are the key drivers of the revolution,' says Kjell Nordström. 'The result is the emergence of a radically different society, new ways of working and new ways of disorganizing work.'

> When it comes to gen e they are defiantly and definitely on message

Karl Marx was right not because Nordström and Ridderstråle have a lingering penchant for Communism but simply because economic capital is now owned by the workers. 'Perfectly formed and individually owned, the human brain is overpowering the traditional means of production – raw material, hard labour and capital. Try to think of one major, innovative organization which is brawn based,' says Nordström.

Their antidote is 'funky business' in which diversity, innovation, uncertainty and change are constantly sought out – and capitalized on. 'Don't expect too much innovation at a company where 90 per cent of the employees have the same gender, are about the same age, come from a similar educational background, and dress in the same way,' says Jonas Ridderstråle, adding, 'even if they go on bi-annual strategy conferences to the Mediterranean or the Alps to be really creative, wild, and crazy.'

In the future, predict Nordström and Ridderstråle, companies will compete on an entirely different basis. They point, for example, to the importance of 'economies of the soul'. 'Economies of scale and skill will not suffice. We must start competing on feelings and fantasy,' says Ridderstråle, going on to sound the death knell for business governed by rationality. 'If there is an excess of everything from components to companies and products to people, success will rest with attracting the emotional rather than the rational customer and colleague.'

> Emotions rule

Emotions rule. 'People expect good stuff. They have become used to great value for money. And they can get that from almost all companies around the world. So, being great is no longer good enough. Customer satisfaction is not enough. To succeed we have to surprise people. We have to attract and addict them. Attention is all,' say the shaven-headed duo. 'Emotion and imagination are the last taboos. To succeed, businesses must exploit them.'

> Nordström and Ridderstråle are dedicatedly European in outlook: gen e personified

Nordström's and Ridderstråle's growing following and increasing impact may sound the death knell for the American management model espoused for so long by the gurus. Nordström and Ridderstråle are dedicatedly European in outlook: gen e personified.

executive gold

Managing the geeks is really a side issue in the power shifts underway in the business world. More critical is the entire issue of executive talent. Revolutionary teachings suggest that the best way to destroy an institution is from within. Many gen e stars are defecting from big business to join the revolution.

There are already signs of talent shortages at the top of US companies. One major US public company anticipates that it will lose 60 per cent of its executives within the next three years. Another talks of 40 per cent to 50 per cent walking through the door. These companies only hint at a crisis facing corporate America: forecasts show that a dearth of executive talent could be a serious problem not just for the next few years, but for the first few decades of the new millennium.

Once upon a time, an orderly line of ready-made executive replacements stood in the wings. Now, the corporate corridors are empty. Thanks to downsizing and an ageing executive population, tomorrow's leaders are already yesterday's men.

Couple these trends with the skills demanded of executives in a global market

> Many gen e stars are defecting from big business to join the revolution

> Once upon a time, an orderly line of ready-made executive replacements stood in the wings. Now, the corporate corridors are empty

and the rise of gen e, and the implications of a talent shortage take on more urgency.

'Demographics mean that there are a lot of people nearing retirement age. Downsizing has meant that companies no longer tend to have developmental roles, like assistant or deputy jobs, from which people were traditionally promoted,' says William C. Byham, president and CEO of Development Dimensions International, a Bridgeville, Pennsylvania, firm that specializes in HR issues. 'At the same time, the experience, qualifications and skills needed to become a senior executive have increased.'[61]

A number of trends suggest that the talent shortfall may be no mere blip on the radar screen; the problem could be with us for decades to come. Three factors, in particular, threaten to exacerbate the situation in the next few years.

First, and in many ways most seriously, the demand for executives appears to be moving in the opposite direction of supply. Remember the demographic time bomb that everyone was talking about back in the 1980s? It didn't go away when the magazine articles halted and now it may be ready to detonate. Demographic predictions suggest that in the USA the number of 35 to 44 year olds – the traditional executive talent pool – will fall by 15 per cent between 2000 and 2015, while the number of 45 to 54 year olds – the current senior executive population – will rise.

The demographic alarm bells date back to the post-World War II baby boom. The baby boomers created a surplus of middle managers in the late 1980s. Now they are creating an ageing workforce – and an ageing executive population. By 2000 there will be more US workers in their late forties than in their late twenties. The number of 40 to 59 year olds in the USA, which stood at 53 million in 1990, will reach 73 million by 2000 and 83 million in 2010. Add in factors like a booming stock market, which is boosting retirement nest eggs, and there are an awful lot of people eyeing condos in Florida.

'The American labor force will shrink in the middle,' says Paul Wallace, author of *Agequake*,[62] which examines demographic trends. 'The baby-boom echo and immigration mean that the US does not face youth deficits. Even so, the bulging portion of the labour force will consist of people over 50. If companies are increasingly looking to younger executives, there will be a problem.'[63]

The negative implications of broad demographic statistics are backed by the findings of surveys. A 1998 study by the management consultants McKinsey and Co., covering nearly 6,000 managers in 77 companies, cautioned that the battle to recruit talented people was already intensifying. The McKinsey report, appropriately entitled *The War for Talent*, concluded: 'Many American companies are already suffering a shortage of executive talent.' The research found that 'three-quarters of corporate officers surveyed said their companies had "insufficient talent sometimes" or were "chronically talent-short across the board".'[64]

Aside from demographics, the second factor in the escalating talent shortage is that companies expect more from their executives these days. Complex global markets require more sophisticated management skills, including international sensitivity, cultural fluency, technological literacy, entrepreneurial flair and, most critically, leadership. The proliferation of business school educated managers, especially MBAs, suggests that executives are better trained than ever before. The trouble is that business schools are good at turning out business analysts but have a more questionable record in producing leaders.

> Who wants to work for a faceless corporation when you can make more money and have more fun working for an exciting upstart?

For large companies, the third factor fuelling an executive dearth is the rise of many high-potential small and midsize companies. For the first time, big companies have to compete with – and provide career opportunities and earnings on a par with – their smaller brethren. A host of high-tech startups, especially internet-based businesses, are likely to draw off a growing proportion of high-fliers who might otherwise have joined the blue chips. Who wants to work for a faceless corporation when you can make more money and have more fun working for an exciting upstart?

> The final ingredient in this is the simple fact that gen e simply do not see their futures within large organizations. Period

The final ingredient in this is the simple fact that gen e simply do not see their futures within large organizations. Period.

All of these factors point to an escalation of the recruitment war. 'While we have no experience of a shortage of executive talent, there is no doubt that recruitment will become more difficult in the future. There will be more competition and recruitment will be a bigger item on the in-house agenda,' says John Hughes, manager of executive recruiting at Wal-Mart.[65]

There appears little doubt that attracting the best and brightest will become much harder for established companies. 'There will continue to be, for the foreseeable future, greater demand than supply of the best people – the most knowledgeable, skilled, innovative, experienced, entrepreneurial, creative, risk-taking supertalent,' says Bruce Tulgan, founder of Rainmaker Thinking. 'Every business leader and manager in every organization I talk with says that they are spending more time, energy and money on recruiting at all levels.'[66]

Leadership guru Warren Bennis, distinguished professor of leadership at the University of Southern California and co-author of *Co-Leaders*, has firsthand experience of the problems now encountered. 'I've recently been helping out a high-powered research centre to find a president. The salary is $500,000 plus a house, car and driver, all the perks, and they can't find anyone who the researchers feel is adequate scientifically and who wants to manage,' Bennis laments. 'The more we move into knowledge-based, technically based organizations – which we clearly are – the scarcer the top leadership talent.'[67]

Other signs should give executives and their employers pause for thought. For one thing, the turnover of senior executives is high. The upper-middle reaches of US corporations are coming to resemble a game of musical chairs, where the music gets faster and faster and chairs are left emptier for longer.

Research conducted by the Center for Creative Leadership (CCL) in Greensboro, North Carolina, and the executive search firm Manchester Partners International found that 40 per cent of new executive hires fail within the first 18 months on the job. As the research report states, they are being 'terminated for poor performance, performing significantly below expectations, or voluntarily resigning from the position'.

With shortages either existing or inevitable in many companies, along with a widespread inability to identify or retain the most suitable executives – a point confirmed by the CCL research – it is surprising how muted the corporate response has been. An eerie silence resonates in boardrooms – the sort of silence you imagine on board the *Titanic* just before she struck ice. Corporate America is in denial.

The implications of the talent gap are many. One of the clearest is that the executive development system is failing. Talented executives are not being produced in substantial numbers with the skills now required.

> An eerie silence resonates in boardrooms – the sort of silence you imagine on board the *Titanic* just before she struck ice. Corporate America is in denial

John Quelch, himself recruited from Harvard in 1998 to become Dean of London Business School, one of Europe's top business schools, believes the proliferation of MBAs and other management qualifications means the management population is better trained than ever before, particularly in hard analytical skill areas. But those skills do not necessarily translate into the executive talent required by leading companies. According to Quelch, the problem is one of leadership.

'There's not so much a shortage of management talent as of leadership talent,' he says. 'The basic technical training managers need is more widespread. But leadership skills are in short supply. This has become a major constraint on the speed with which multinational companies can expand. The additional problem in the US is the high level of entrepreneurial opportunities which draw off a considerable amount of talent from the Fortune 500 companies.'[68]

Randall White, director of RPW Executive Development in Greensboro, North Carolina, takes a more philosophical view of the talent shortage, pointing to development as the key issue. 'This is a periodic crisis,' he says. 'Depending on how you define it, we have been in this situation for a number of years. I believe it is a continuous state. If you think about it, there could never be enough talent available. How and when talent is developed is perhaps a more important question.'[69]

The point, according to White, is that most large companies are not prepared to develop their executive potential to benefit the wider business community. They develop executives for their own needs. Period. As a result, there is little excess capacity within the business world as a whole for the hard times ahead. The situation, he believes, is worsening. 'Bench strength remains an issue,' he says. 'There are still few companies that are net exporters of executives – that is, they develop more than they need. GE is one company which does so, but there are few others. Years ago, Westinghouse, Merrill Lynch, Chase Manhattan and others were all net exporters of talent. Also, the military has dried up as a place to grow and test talent. While some may question how big a source it ever was, it should be remembered that military academies are really leadership training academies.'

attracting gen e

For all the shortages and perceived lack of talent, some simple truths are at work. First, talented gen e executives are likely to be lured to companies that have a reputation for successfully developing people. Talent attracts talent and gen e attracts gen e. This means that the gap between the haves and have-nots – companies with a track record of developing and retaining talented managers versus those whose reputation in this area is less impressive – is likely to widen. While some companies are already dealing from a shrinking executive deck, others are likely to continue to turn up executive trumps.

> Talent attracts talent and gen e attracts gen e

According to Chip R. Bell, senior partner at Performance Research Associates based in its Dallas office, talent shortages will not be a problem for trailblazing companies, but will add to the woes of their less dynamic brethren. 'Among the winning organizations – like Sun Microsystems, Dell, Amazon.com, Southwest Airlines – there will be plenty of talent. But too many organizations value control over creativity, incremental improvement rather than breakthroughs,' says Bell. At a time when there is a premium on creativity and the ability to lead and manage major changes, an emphasis on control is unlikely to nurture executives with the right skills for the

> 'The key word is not top or executive; the key word is talent'

future. The key word is not top or executive; the key word is talent, Bell adds. 'Too many organizations are managed (not led) by administrative babysitters who lack the courage to be bold, the imagination to be innovative and the compassion to focus on culture. True effective talent focuses on creating a learning organization to keep associates sharp, adaptive and multitalented.'[70]

Bill Byham of DDI suggests that companies take three steps. First, identify people who are about to retire and try to keep them on – by offering more flexible and attractive sunset career options including part-time work, consultancy and advisory roles.

Second, shore up the company's selection systems, plugging the holes where talented managers leak out of the organization. Systems and individuals need to recognize that more money or promotion may not be the key to retention if someone wants time out to pursue other interests: for example, through active succession planning, a more tailored approach to career development and sabbaticals.

Third, develop a talent pool by creating and maintaining ongoing dialogue with former executives, headhunters and other strategic partners including business schools. Companies need to identify the people they can 'fast track to senior management positions', Byham says.

Perhaps the most obvious solution is to recruit from a broader base. Smart companies will recognize that the male Anglo-Saxon power trip is over. For all the talk of women and ethnic groups making their way into top positions, research shows they are hugely underrepresented. Research from the Kelley School of Business at Indiana University, for example, shows that the number of women in executive positions in the USA is now lower than it was ten years ago. In 1987, there were 11 female directors at Fortune 500 companies; by 1997, there were just eight. The number of women CEOs in these companies was two in 1987 and remains the same a decade later. It is tempting to say that if corporate America continues to recruit from less than half of the total population, then it deserves to be held to ransom by star managers demanding higher salaries and better terms.

> Smart companies will recognize that the male Anglo-Saxon power trip is over

The solution, according to McKinsey, lies in elevating talent management to 'a burning corporate priority'. This means creating and refining a value proposition for your company that draws in prospective managers. Senior management must have a persuasive answer as to why a talented employee should work for their company rather than a competitor.

John Hughes of Wal-Mart maps his company's value proposition with practised ease: 'We offer a great deal. We are an international company – that's a strong selling point especially because we're expanding internationally – with a great culture. Our leadership is down to earth, approachable and open minded. More folks are now looking at that total picture rather than simply considering finance. They don't just look at the job but at what they can grow into. People aren't as loyal. We have an extremely strong culture and that is a great retention tool.'

> If corporate America continues to recruit from less than half of the total population, then it deserves to be held to ransom by star managers demanding higher salaries and better terms

The race is on to become an employer of choice, and that race must be led from the top. Recruitment and retention should become full responsibilities of the board as prospecting for executive talent becomes a business imperative.

> The race is on to become an employer of choice, and that race must be led from the top

There are precedents in Silicon Valley. In the software industry, the fight for top-notch people already requires personal intervention from the very top. At Microsoft, Bill Gates regards hiring smart people – 'high IQ people', as he calls them – as one of his primary roles. It is not uncommon for Gates to take a personal interest in the recruitment process. If a particularly talented programmer needs a little extra persuasion to sign up, Gates will happily pick up the phone himself to clinch the hire. As talent becomes more scarce, CEOs will have to man the recruitment lines.

One problem with this development is that senior executives may have trouble understanding what motivates gen e, and that may lessen their ability to recognize top prospects, or to play a role in recruitment. (They also may be unhappy about taking part in what is traditionally the HR function's job.) A CEO looking to cash in stock options in a couple of years may not connect with the new generation of executives who value employability and personal development more highly than mere money.

Of course the easiest solution to a talent shortage is to look outside. Forget development. Forget succession. In the short term, companies will simply look to import executives with the right skills. 'Looking outside for talent is riskier and more expensive,' warns Byham. He is right, but the recruitment industry is likely to be one of the chief beneficiaries of the talent shortage. In a crisis, the easy option always flourishes. Headhunters and top-level selection firms will be much in demand as they seek out executive talent from throughout the world.

Research from the Economist Intelligence Unit in 1999 indicates that the global executive search market is now worth in the region of $7 billion to $8 billion. Nancy Garrison Jenn, market expert and author of *Executive Search in Europe*,[71] predicts that if the market continues to grow at its current rate it will exceed $10 billion by 2000 – just about the time that executive shortages really start to bite. The search for outside executives will become more global as companies feel the pinch, according to Richard Wall, managing partner responsible for European investment banking at Heidrick and Struggles, the world's second largest headhunter, which operates mostly at the board level and just below. 'We are already seeing a shortage of future leaders. That is clear right now. There are not that many people who are able to operate across continents and right across organizations. We are finding more and more companies have to go global with their searches,' Wall says.[72]

Fishing in foreign ponds, where the effects of demographics are less dramatic, is at best a short-term solution. As shortages in the USA persist, there will be a ripple effect – shortages in the countries being poached from. In the end, aggressive poaching leads to soaring salary levels, and companies on the losing end of employee raids have little incentive to invest in staff development when that investment is likely to walk out the door.

the new power elite

P ower shifts. The gen e reality is that recruitment firms are sitting pretty. So, too, are gen e. 'It will mean that true executive talent will have their choice of the plum roles,' says Bell of Performance Research Associates. 'It will mean the old-style administrator will become in less demand and will have to settle for positions below mahogany row. It will also spark a redefinition of what it means to be an executive.' Executives who have built their careers on their ability to rifle through their in-tray quickly and handle paperwork face fast approaching extinction. Trouble is that the new skills of the executive are more ethereal and elusive – motivation, mentoring, coaching.

For the select few, the world will be their oyster. (For the rest, a clam.) Have talent, will travel. 'Geography will be much less important in future. A new pattern of graduates and post-graduates is emerging,' says Wall of Heidrick and Struggles. 'But more to the point, there is much less of a country focus to jobs. Executives are more willing to look across borders. I think we are going to see a workforce which is much more transient, moving between companies and even continents.'

Power shifts. The gen e reality is that recruitment firms are sitting pretty. So, too, are gen e

The new skills of the executive are more ethereal and elusive – motivation, mentoring, coaching

Gen e will be in demand and will be able to attract substantial salary and remuneration packages. In effect, corporate power will be concentrated in the hands of the few. 'What is critical in the firm of the future is not so much the core competencies as the core competents,' predicts Jonas Ridderstråle, assistant professor at the Stockholm School of Economics. 'These walking monopolies will stay as long as the company can offer them something they want. When that is no longer the case, they will leave.'

> Gen e will be in demand and will be able to attract substantial salary and remuneration packages

Ridderstråle points to a growing array of supporting evidence. Bill Gates has reflected that if twenty of Microsoft's key people were to leave, the company would risk bankruptcy. In a study by the Corporate Leadership Council, a computer firm recognized 100 'core competents' out of 16,000 employees; a software company had 10 out of 11,000; and a transportation group deemed 20 of its 33,000 employees as really critical.

So few, yet so powerful. According to Randall E. Stross, professor of business at San José State University and a research fellow at Stanford University: 'In the software industry, a single programmer's intellectual resources, through commercial alchemy, can create entire markets where none existed before. Compare the cumulative worldwide gross revenues of the studio that captures the next Steven Spielberg [with] the rival who has to settle for the second-round draft pick. Differences separating the rewards generated by the top tier vs. the second tier are geometric, not arithmetic.'

At the top of the organization, the difference is likely to be exponential. The superstar CEOs will be able to call the shots – demanding and receiving high salaries and taking on the jobs that interest them most. When that interest fades, they will leave. Already, we see interim executives – senior managers right up to CEO level who step in on a temporary basis – Apple's Steve Jobs being the best known example.

Indeed, some suggest that we are expecting too much from senior managers in general, and CEOs in particular. Having created impossible expectations, companies are surprised that their appointees fail to live up to those expectations.

Little wonder there are talent shortages. Renaissance men and women are rare. 'Leadership in a modern organization is highly complex, and it is increasingly difficult – sometimes impossible – to find all the necessary traits in a single person,' says Ridderstråle. 'In the future, we will see leadership groups rather than individual leaders.'

All of this means that 'Show me the money', the demand made famous in the movie *Jerry Maguire*, could have new resonance for top executives in the next few years. In the film a professional athlete delivered that line to his wheeler-dealer agent, played by Tom Cruise. How long before top executives start hiring such agents for themselves?

Not long at all, if Leigh Steinberg has anything to do with it. Said to be the model for Tom Cruise's character, Steinberg runs a law firm, Steinberg and Moorad, that represents more than one hundred athletes and negotiates multi-million-dollar deals for some of America's best known sports stars – including Troy Aikman, Drew Bledsoe, Warren Moon and Ryan Leaf. The news that Steinberg is now exploring ways of expanding his business to include negotiating on behalf of top business talent should be enough to strike terror into the hearts of recruiters everywhere. The CEO agency with gen e stars is surely only a matter of time.

Steinberg plays hard ball. He believes that negotiating is a contact sport to be enjoyed by everyone. His approach is that it is a part of everyday life and should be handled in a professional way – with clear focus and a principled philosophy. 'The goal', he insists, 'is not to destroy the other side, but to find the most profitable way to complete a deal that works for both sides.' This involves the mastery of a number of lessons, including: everyone is a negotiator – we all negotiate all the time, but many of us still have a fundamental fear of negotiation; negotiate with yourself – a vital step in any deal is introspection; understanding what you want out of the situation; and move from your values to your value – once you understand your own values, you have to understand your value in the world.

Finally, whether it's signing football jerseys to cement a multi-million-dollar contract or just having a beer together after obtaining a salary increase, Steinberg advocates including some kind of ceremonial ritual – to complete the deal.

Steinberg – or even the idea of a CEO agency – may be just the shock the corporate world needs to start taking talent shortages seriously. According to Rainmaker's Tulgan, the process is already under way: 'More and more of the best talent are acting like free agents,' he says. 'Many have consultancies of one – they sell some unique skill or knowledge on the open market. Many are happy to represent themselves. As agents emerge to represent these free-agent knowledge workers, such agents will be successful to the extent that they are able to demonstrate they add significant value to the equation. Already, plenty of executive recruiters play a similar role, as do some of the consulting firms that pull in outside independent consultants to work on key projects.'

what if?

When Dave Allan and Matt Kingdon left their marketing jobs at Unilever to set up their own business in 1992 they had one simple goal: to create the best innovation company in the world. From experience, they knew they had their best ideas away from the office.

So they turned the office into a home from home, complete with rugs, armchairs and a table football game, hold client meetings in the kitchen and even run a company slate at the local pub. Such eccentric behaviour may sound more like student high jinx than a serious business, but at ?What If! they are hardened marketing professionals who have developed a multi-million-dollar business from harnessing the power of human imagination.

> They turned the office into a home from home, complete with rugs, armchairs and a table football game, hold client meetings in the kitchen and even run a company slate at the local pub

They recognized the need to help free the imagination and encourage innovation in all companies. They were joined by Kristina Murrin, a former brand manager at Procter and Gamble and Daz Rudkin, another ex-Unilever marketing manager.

They describe the management style as the 'serious relaxed business' – something that seems to appeal to big corporates. Their client list includes Heinz,

Colgate Palmolive, British Airways, Cadbury-Schweppes, ICI, Pepsi Co, Lever Brothers, Thomson Holidays and Royal Mail.

Allan uses the analogy of an oil company – 'There are two sides to an oil company. There's the 249,000 people in suits and overalls who exploit the assets of the company today, then there are the people on the exploration side – hairy-kneed, hairy-faced men who search the world for oil – "gold" – and then as soon as they've found it say "OK, where next?"'

It's not just oil companies that need the pioneering spirit, he says. All businesses require people to prospect for the future. Most, however, lose the ability to do so as they get larger. 'There's nowhere to play in a big company,' he explains; 'there's no room for experimentation or invention.'

That's where ?What If! comes in. It helps clients explore the frontier between the corporate world – where products are developed – and the real world where consumers actually use them.

For a fee ranging from £10,000 to £250,000, the company works on projects with clients to develop – or invent – new products or services. The approach is summed up by the term 'Madness and Measure'. Often, this involves challenging the way companies look at problems. For example, the company has a special arrangement with people living in certain streets in London. 'We take clients there and say "Knock on any door in this street, and the people who live here will let you into their homes,"' Allan explains. "You can see how they use your products and hear what they think of them." It's very powerful because they see with their own eyes.'

Clients were so impressed that a number asked the company to help them develop their in-house capability. Out of this grew a second string to the business bow. It involves helping companies identify and overcome the internal barriers – including attitudes and behaviours, physical environment and the way they are structured – which prevent them unleashing the latent inventiveness of their own people.

Between the two activities, the company now has fifty-plus full-time employees. 'Have fun to encourage fun' is also part of the management philosophy. As well as a profit share scheme, the company subscribes to a range of initiatives designed to make staff 'feel good!'. These include paid-for visits to the office from a yoga teacher; deliveries of fresh fruit; and company accounts at local pubs – where employees go on a Friday night safe in the knowledge that the company appreciates their work and wants to buy them a drink.

outsider's paradise

Power shifts. Upstarts rule

P ower shifts. Upstarts rule. The new economy is an outsider's paradise. An anarchist dream. It favours the new breed of entrepreneur over the suits of the corporate establishment.

According to IDC, small businesses (2 to 20 employees), solo entrepreneurs and telecommuters currently make up a universe of 41.3 million in the USA which is expected to grow to 51.6 million by 2002. The annual buying power of this group exceeds $100 billion. In the USA, SoHo (small office/home office) use of the internet leapt to 41.2 per cent in 1998, up from 19.7 per cent in 1996. Small businesses are overwhelmingly accepting the internet as critical to the management and operation of their businesses – enabling them to compete more equitably with larger companies. The top 10 home-based businesses are:

- Business consulting and services
- Computer services and programming
- Financial consulting and services
- Marketing and advertising

- Medical practices and services

- Graphics and visual arts

- Public relations

- Real estate

- Writing

- Independent sales.[73]

Nowhere is the power of outsiders clearer than on the internet. Most of the content of corporate sites has been at best tailored electronic versions of materials which have existed in different formats. Companies, particularly in Europe, are still struggling to find the right tone of voice for their websites. This is partly due to the newness of the medium and the requirement to replace static one-directional communications with dynamic interactive ones.

> Nowhere is the power of outsiders clearer than on the internet

One of the most consistent threats to the Clinton administration has been the *Drudge Report* – which *Brill's Content* describes as a 'flamboyantly provocative, often outrageous internet news compendium that is roiling the elite journalistic establishment all the way to the president of the United States'. President Clinton allegedly calls it the Sludge Report. In one month alone, following the breaking of the Monica Lewinsky story, the Drudge site received over six million visits – 29,000 from the White House.

The role of the computer hacker is literally to break into the organization. Interestingly, a number of former hackers now have legitimate businesses advising their former victims. Gen e are hacking into the markets of big business. In a business environment, the net threatens to throw out not only the rules of the game but the whole game itself. Businesses which took years to form and to build trade, customer relations, quality assurance and the like see three-year-old organizations float for billions of dollars on the exchange. Look at the speed at which Java built up a customer base.

> Gen e are hacking into the markets of big business

The internet is inherently revolutionary. In fact, as Harvard Business School's Professor William Sahlman points out, that is what the new economy is all about – companies attacking the status quo and entrenched players.

From the perspective of personal power – it breaks the grip that the corporation once had on knowledge workers (whether they are on the inside or the outside of the organization) and sets them on their way to accruing personal power and wealth for themselves. Freed from their corporate cells, gen e are able to take flight in cyberspace.

> Freed from their corporate cells, gen e are able to take flight in cyberspace

The fall of entry barriers has created some unexpected new stars. Take the Hollywood film industry, a powerful and market-led sector which is being threatened by Harry Knowles, a single, overweight film buff who posts film reviews from his bedroom in Austin, Texas.[74] No one is more surprised than Harry. The site is called www.aint-it-cool-news.com which seeks to give advance warning on whether an upcoming film release is good or not. In its own inimitably crass words: 'Ain't It Cool News is a Harry Knowles production bringing you the latest in movie, TV, comic and other coolness that's got Hollywood's panties in a bunch.'

www.aint-it-cool-news.com   **virtual visit**

As Harry describes his own growing fame/infamy, so also the network of informal alliances begins to grow around him: 'Wow, here ya are! Well my little site keeps on growing, much to my shock. As you will find I attempt to cover all stages of development of the films that you and I look forward to, without the "studio line" clouding our judgement. This site works with the help of people like you. Now everyone has a chance to be a "spy", because inevitably at some point there will be a moment where Hollywood enters your life, before it enters ours. If you see something filming, a trailer, an advance screening or something I can't even imagine. If you read a script, hear something from behind the scenes … Well let me know. I try to cover it all, and you, your neighbors, boss, or even the local weatherman … well y'all make this site special. It's your eyes, ears and opinions, well … we're making a difference. Also we do cover the "uncool" films, we warn each other of the Hollywood powered Nuclear Bombs, and the super cool products.'

Penetrate the dreadful Beverley Hillbillies argot and relentless bonhomie and you may note the use of the word 'spies'. Harry openly exhorts a show of subversion to the multi-billion-dollar Hollywood industry, an industry which test-markets its products (particularly the saccharined endings) on focus groups, adapting the final product to consumer needs.

Harry's warnings to site users have made him a target of Hollywood vitriol, and other attention, as was demonstrated by what happened when *Jackie Brown* came out. This was the much anticipated movie from Quentin Tarantino – responsible for *Pulp Fiction*. *Jackie Brown* was a different product: less reliant on violence, black humour and a stylish soundtrack. Instead it focused on real people caught in a world of small-time crime who have to cope with the growing realization that life is progressing and they have less to show for it. *Jackie Brown* was hailed as a more 'mature' film, but was receiving mixed reviews from influential critics – far less ecstatic than for *Pulp Fiction*.

Such is the power of Harry Knowles's website that he and his family were taken out on the town in Austin by Tarantino and his associates. Although Harry does not see it as such, such 'entertainment' could be viewed as a slick piece of lobbying by Tarantino on behalf of his own film. Soon after, *Jackie Brown* received a glowing account by Harry on his site.

Such is the enormous investment in films that a few failures can threaten the financial health of the studio. This makes powerful media such as aint-it-cool-news absolutely key in determining how the weathervane of popular opinion will swing. Harry has been keen to distance himself from the commercial interests which might influence the more mainstream reviewers. He stresses that the banner advertising in his site (the movie review section is currently sponsored by Sprint) is unsolicited, does not influence him and has the benefit of keeping the site free of charge to users.

Outsiders like Harry are where the power now lies. Unpredictable outsiders call the corporate tune. Challenging complacent market leaders, slothful incumbents, is gen e.

One of the best examples of this comes from the airline easyJet; easyJet is one of the most interesting and bravest of entrepreneurial adventures. The airline began life at the end of 1995 from the UK's Luton airport. In summer 1997 easyJet owner Stelios Haji-Ioannou signed a deal with Boeing for 12 new aircraft costing $500 million.

The easyJet story is one of imagination and no little bravery. The lessons for the fledgling entrepreneur are many. Most notably, find a role model. Haji-Ioannou flew with Southwest Airlines in the USA and was converted. Southwest is renowned for its frills-free service and remarkable corporate culture. This was the basic model.

> Unpredictable outsiders call the corporate tune. Challenging complacent market leaders, slothful incumbents, is gen e

Rather than exporting the Southwest model wholesale, Haji-Ioannou introduced various adaptations. For example, he cut out travel agents – easyJet is reliant on direct sales. He also had a very clear idea of who his potential customers would be. The market, he decided, was travellers who were cost conscious. These were split into three groups: travellers visiting relatives, leisure travellers making brief trips and managers and executives from small firms. Then easyJet worked at making the process of purchasing a ticket and travelling as simple as possible. Booking a seat was simple – no tickets, no assigned seats, minimum check-in times. The company concentrated on supplying the planes, cabin crew and pilots and on sales and marketing. Other activities were outsourced with suppliers being rigourously rated against a matrix.

Now comes the hardest part. Competition is increasing with a flood of direct competitors. Keeping the entrepreneurial spirit alive is demanding. 'All I need to do now is find six million people a year to fly on my new planes,' Haji-Ioannou has reflected.

the beauty of virginity

'I believe there is almost no limit to what a brand can do, but only if used properly,' says Richard Branson, founder of the Virgin empire. In the past two decades, Richard Branson has provided a bearded template for gen e. His entrepreneurial brilliance lies in retaining the perspective of an outsider while playing a mainstream game.

> In the past two decades, Richard Branson has provided a bearded template for gen e

Branson's greatest achievement, to date, is to create what is arguably the world's first universal brand. Other famous names have become synonymous with the product they adorn: Hoover vacuum cleaners, Coca-Cola and Levi Strauss to name just a few. But Virgin

www.virgin.co.uk   **virtual visit**

is alone among western brands in its ability to transcend products. Never before has a single brand been so successfully deployed across such a diverse range of goods and services. It has been used to sell everything from condoms to financial services, bridal gowns to the Sex Pistols.

The most important aspect of the Virgin brand proposition is its credibility among its market segment. Just as existing Virgin products and services provide credibility for new offerings, the relationship between the Virgin family could also work in reverse. If the image were to become tarnished by association with a shoddy product, a poor service or an offering that was a rip-off, then the standing of the wider Virgin brand could be damaged.

Yet despite its remarkable success, Branson would have us believe that none of it was planned. He gives the impression that the Virgin phenomenon is one of those odd things that happen to people sometimes. This is part of the Branson mystique. He makes it look and sound so simple.

'When we came up with the name "Virgin" instead of "Slipped Disc" Records for our record company in the winter of 1969, I had some vague idea of the name being catchy and applying to lots of other products for young people. It would have been interesting to have tracked the success of the Virgin companies or otherwise if we had called the company Slipped Disc Records. Slipped Disc Condoms might not have worked as well.'[75]

The quip is typical of a man who has lived his whole life like some big adventure. An outspoken critic of business schools and management theory, Branson likes to portray himself as the ordinary man on the street (despite his comfortable middle-class origins). He is the small guy who outsmarts the big guys. His account of how the famous Virgin logo came to be is typical of the way things seem to happen at Virgin.

'When Virgin Records became successful we followed our instinct,' Branson explains. 'Initially the music reflected the "hippy" era and our logo of a naked lady back to back reflected that too. Then when Punk came along we felt we needed a crisper image ... Rather than spending a fortune coming up with the new image, I was talking to our graphic designer one day explaining what we wanted and he threw on the floor his doodling – the now famous Virgin signature – which I fortunately picked up on the way to the loo.'

It sounds so casual, but the words mask an extraordinary entrepreneurial mind, one that has reinvented business to fit the times he lives in. Today, Branson is the driving force at the centre of a web of somewhere between 150 and 200 companies, employing more than 8,000 people in 26 countries. His commercial interests span travel, hotels, consumer goods, computer games, music and airlines. You can even buy a Virgin pension or investment plan.

Financial services is a far cry from the adolescent record label that helped put Punk on the map in the 1980s, with a controversially named album by the Sex Pistols. By then, Virgin had already won the respect of the hippy generation with 'Tubular Bells', from a young unknown artist called Mike Oldfield. 'Never Mind the Bollocks' was the perfect product to establish the Virgin brand with a new generation of spiky-haired teenagers. Branson had created a new fusion of rebellion and business – and discovered a unique new brand proposition. He has been repeating the formula ever since.

Originally aimed at younger people, as Branson has matured so too has the Virgin appeal. 'Four years ago we crossed over into appealing to their parents', he says. 'Now we're moving into pensions and life insurance. We haven't quite reached funeral parlours. But we have to be careful we don't lose the kids. I'd like people to feel most of their needs in life can be filled by Virgin. The absolutely critical thing is we must never let them down.'[76] By the mid-1990s, the Virgin name seemed to be everywhere. So ubiquitous had the Virgin brand become that hardly a day seemed to go by without seeing a grinning Richard Branson launching some new Virgin product or service. The famous flying V logo was emblazoned on aircraft, megastore and cinema fronts and was about to make its debut on cola cans.

The activity prompted some to question whether the Virgin brand was being diluted. Those who understood what he was about, however, recognized that what Branson had created was an entirely new kind of brand proposition. John Murphy, chairman of the famous brand consultancy Interbrand, for example, observed that: 'Unless they poison someone or start applying the brand to inappropriate products such as pension funds or photocopiers, I doubt whether the Virgin brand will ever be diluted.' Little did Murphy know that by 1996 Virgin Direct would be offering financial services – including pensions.

Branson has acknowledged time and time again that the most vital asset Virgin has is the reputation of its brand. Put the Virgin name on any product that doesn't come up to scratch and the whole company is brought into disrepute. 'Our customers trust us,' he says simply.

The Branson philosophy then is: look after your brand and it will last. There is, however, and always has been, a tension at the heart of the Virgin brand. For all his unquestioned emphasis on the integrity of the Virgin name, one of Branson's personal characteristics – that has become a strand of what Virgin stands for – is a certain restlessness. He has an insatiable desire to take risks and explore new areas. It is in his blood that Branson has to be constantly expanding the borders of the empire. Yet it is vital to do so without damaging the good name of the company. This creates something of a dilemma. It is one of which Branson is well aware: 'We are expanding and growing our use of the brand,' he says, 'but are always mindful of the fact that we should only put it on products and services that fit – or will fit – our very exacting criteria.'

In recent years, he has thought long and hard about what the Virgin brand stands for. He believes the reputation which the company has built up is based on five key factors: value for money, quality, reliability, innovation and an indefinable, but nonetheless palpable, sense of fun. (Another, slightly snappier, version of the Virgin brand values is: genuine and fun, contemporary and different, consumers' champion, and first class at business-class price.)[77]

In a classic piece of reverse engineering, these are now the brand values that Branson applies when considering new business ventures. He says any new product or service must fulfil, or have the prospect of fulfilling in the future, the following criteria:

- it must represent the best quality
- it must be innovative
- it must be good value for money
- it must be challenging to existing alternatives, and
- it must add a sense of fun or cheekiness.

Virgin claims that nine out of ten projects it considers are potentially very profitable, but if they don't fit with the group's values they are rejected.[78] But, says Branson: 'If an idea satisfies at least four of these five criteria, we'll usually take a serious look at it.'

e working

free at last

Power shifts and the new economy are already having an effect on the way we work. Work is changing. And, once again, it's not just in Palo Alto. In the 1990s an unprecedented range of people took control of their own work, liberating themselves from the daily grind of nine-to-five jobs. For them singing the company song lost its appeal. Under their breath, many were already humming Frank Sinatra's refrain 'My Way'. 'I was never really a banker. I was an entrepreneur working for a bank. I remember I was in some boring meeting in Portugal, and I just thought this isn't what I want to do with my life,' says bagel queen Danielle Downing.

In the USA, tens of millions of people have now freed themselves from corporate control. According to Daniel Pink, formerly Vice-President Gore's chief speechwriter, there are 14 million self-employed Americans. There are 8.3 million independent contractors and a further 2.3 million who work for temporary agencies. This adds up to around 25 million free agents, he says, 'people who move from project to project and who work on their own, sometimes for months, sometimes for days'.

Many of those who have left the corporate fold actually find greater security in self-employment. The redundancies of recent years mean that being on their own no longer holds the fear it once did. A marketing consultant recounts how a bank was dubious about giving a loan to someone without a real job. 'If one of my clients goes away, I'm still going to make my payments,' she explained. 'But if I'm employed by Apple and they let me go, I'm out on the street.' That's gen e logic.

A similar pattern is unfolding in cities around the world. In London, independents working in design, fashion, broadcasting and the internet, for example, now make up 10 per cent of the workforce and generate £50 billion ($82.5 billion) a year in the UK as a whole. That figure is set to rise to £80 billion ($132 billion) in the next decade (6 per cent of the country's GDP).[79] It's a global movement.

'The economics of free agency relate to a basic psychological shift, a tremendous San Andreas Fault between employee and employer,' says futurist Stan Davis. Earthquakes are inevitable.

This change in attitude presents a challenge to today's companies. How can corporations persuade employees to trust them? How do they convince potential employees that they are willing to pursue the employee's agenda as well as their own? The question is whether the corporate world has the will or the imagination to bridge the gap.

'The biggest transformation since the industrial revolution is underway in our nation's workforce,' says the appropriately named Terri Lonier, president of Working Solo Inc, a company that advises companies such as Microsoft, Hewlett-Packard and Apple on how to access and communicate with rapidly growing small businesses.

'SoHo' describes companies with 1 to 20 employees. It is the fastest growing segment of the business community, making up 13 per cent of *Inc* magazine's 1998 Top 500 list. What are the characteristics of the typical US small business? A Dun and Bradstreet survey of companies with fewer than one hundred employees found that the average small business has three employees, generates between $150,000 and $200,000 in revenue each year, operates from 1.3 locations, is privately owned, is not franchised, and has an owner who puts in a 50.4 hour week.

The notion of free agency is integral to the way gen e thinks. More than a statistic, it's a state of mind. Many remain inside or on the periphery of companies, but their mental software is different from that of previous generations. They think for themselves. They think different. Twenty years ago it couldn't have happened. Work has changed.

There are two forces at work. Push and pull.

- The push is the destruction of the notion of a job as a permanent fixture.

- The pull is the move to new organizations and business models as the principal drivers in the creation of wealth.

Together these two forces have accelerated the rise of individualism. Together they represent a potential double whammy to the corporation. New attitudes, new technology and new organizations are now converging to create the environment where gen e can thrive. Generation e has evolved to fit this new environment. Technology, including the internet, plays a part in that. But it's only an enabler. Equally important is their perception of and relationship with employment. Companies have never been so dependent on a few key workers. Gen e are the technology wizards who have brought the corporate world to heel.

Gen e get it. They have grasped the fundamental work reality: if they don't create value – either for themselves or for someone else – then they won't have a job. No amount of corporate cocooning can change that fact of economic life. Being entrepreneurial is an economic necessity. Survival depends on it. The question, then, is do you want to do it for yourself, for a company, or for some other organization?

For a growing number of people, it's a no brainer. Why, after all, would they want to line someone else's pockets? Why would they trust their skills to someone else? Why take that chance?

They are entering the workplace with their own agenda and are not prepared

> The notion of free agency is integral to the way gen e thinks. More than a statistic, it's a state of mind

> New attitudes, new technology and new organizations are now converging to create the environment where gen e can thrive. Generation e has evolved to fit this new environment

> Gen e are the technology wizards who have brought the corporate world to heel

to stick around if their needs are not being met. Companies had the chance to earn the loyalty and respect of their knowledge workers. But companies blew it. It didn't happen overnight. It took time. Shifts in the employment market over the past two decades have had a profound influence on the way people think about work and their relationship to employers. Gen e are the product of that shift.

pez heads

Demand meets supply in cyberspace

From an art deco ashtray to the services of a patent lawyer, online auctions offer the best of all worlds. Demand meets supply in cyberspace. After more than a century of fixed price commerce, online auctions mark a return to more traditional pricing. They mean that market forces can do their thing. Friction is virtually eliminated. Adam Smith would have been ecstatic.

eBay is the dominant player in the online auctions business, with 7.7 million registered users bidding on more than 3 million items. It is that most unusual of beasts, a .com business that makes profits. In fact, eBay has made money from the first month it was launched.

It all began with Pierre Omidyar and a Pez dispenser (one of those candy brick dispensers with a cartoon character's head that tilts back). In 1995, Omidyar's fiancée, now wife, Pam, an avid collector of Pez dispensers, was bemoaning the complexities of doing trades with other Pez heads. Omidyar, already on the way to his first million with eShop, a company he co-founded and that was eventually bought by Microsoft, gave the matter some thought.

The Pez crisis gave him the inspiration for an internet auction site. He did what Silicon Valley folk do in such circumstances, wrote some

www.ebay.com virtual visit

code. Over the Labor Day weekend, he launched Auction Web. The site was supported by a local internet service provider in the San Francisco Bay area. The site's domain name was www.ebay.com. The name stuck.

'What I wanted to do was create a marketplace where everyone had access to the same information,' says Omidyar. Initially, it was a free service listing computer equipment (the Pez heads had to wait a little longer). But it soon attracted so much traffic that Omidyar's monthly internet bill leapt from $30 to $250. Time to start charging: a nominal amount for listing an item (originally 10 cents and still as little as 25 cents today) and a percentage of the final sale price.

The cash amounts it brought in were small – sometimes dimes and nickels taped to cards – but there were a lot of them. eBay took in $1,000 in its first month, more than its running costs. Omidyar first knew he'd struck egold when he offered a broken laser pointer ($30 new) which was destined for the garbage can. He disclosed that it didn't work and started the bidding at $1. A flurry of inexplicable bids carried it to the heady height of $14.

Meanwhile the site continued to double its revenues. It brought in $2,500 in its second month, then $5,000 and then $10,000. Omidyar grasped the significance. 'I said OK, I've got a hobby that's making me more money than my day job. So it might be time to quit the day job,' he recalls.

It was a smart move. Today, eBay is one of the net's top brands, second only to Amazon.com. It ended 1999 with a market value of around $20 billion. Even smarter, some would say, Omidyar brought in the right people at the right time. His first move was to bring in a partner – Jeff Skoll, a friend and Stanford MBA. By 1997, Omidyar had a venture capital firm in sight – Benchmark Capital, whose initial $6.5 million investment is now worth around $4 billion. Then he recruited a CEO. Former Disney marketing executive Meg Whitman was lured away from Hasbro (where she presided over the Mr Potato Head toy line among others) to handle the company's IPO.

'I've obviously tried to push her to the forefront. Meg's the public face of the company.' He prefers to stay in the background. In his own words, he is the 'classic technowonk'. A computer enthusiast in high school and computer science major at Tufts University, he fits the Silicon Valley stereotype. 'I was the typical nerd or geek,' he admits. 'I forget which one is the good one now.'

On 24 September 1998, the IPO offered shares at $18. By the end of the day, the price had spiralled to $47. Omidyar, Skoll, Whitman and the rest of the eBay crew were suddenly rich. When staff heard the news, spontaneous conga lines broke out in the office.

At 32, Omidyar is worth a cool $5 billion depending on eBay's share price. He moved to France, to rediscover his roots (he lived there until he was 4 years old). Since then, eBay has had some ups and downs: a series of site crashes, including a 10-hour glitch in August 1999, and the odd prankster offering bizarre items for sale. One seller offered a kidney for auction – the bidding reached $5.7 million before the company stepped in to pull the plug. Listings for a bazooka and other military equipment were also pulled. Most famously, there was the 17-year-old boy who put his virginity up for sale.

Despite the glitches, eBay looks likely to remain one of the net stars in the future. For buyers, online auctions provide an opportunity to locate and bid on items around the globe. They are assured of the best price because they get to choose the lowest one on offer anywhere. Sellers, meanwhile, ensure the best price available at any given moment. For an industry that's only been going four years, the numbers are impressive: $4.5 billion in sales in 1999 and an estimated $15.1 billion by 2001.[80]

The competition is increasing, however. Amazon added an auction site in early 1999. Yahoo, the most visited site on the web, introduced auctions in 1998. And in September 1999 Microsoft, Dell Computer and some one hundred other companies said they were to link their websites in an auction consortium run by another online auction company, FairMarket.

www.ubid.com virtual visit

There is also a plethora of specialist online auction operators. Among them, ubid.com selling new ovens; and going-going-sold.com, offering used microscopes. There are also online auctions for services.

www.going-going-sold.com virtual visit

Elance.com is the place for the pleasing spectacle of lawyers underbidding each other for assignments to register patents. The list lengthens every day.

But the company that started the bidding and achieved 'first mover' advantage

virtual visit   www.elance.com

is far from going, going, gone. For eBay the prospects remain more than bright. Its slogan 'eBay everywhere', reminiscent of Microsoft's 'a PC on every desk, and in every home', is one that many believe will stand the test of time – that's real time.

e careers

L ook back. During the more stable times of the 1950s and 1960s the careers enjoyed by corporate executives were built on solid foundations. This was the era of corporate man (there was no such thing as corporate woman at this time). Grey-suited and obedient, corporate man was unstintingly loyal to his employer. He spent his life with a single company and rose slowly, but quietly, up the hierarchy.

> Grey-suited and obedient, corporate man was unstintingly loyal to his employer

Implicit to such careers was the understanding that loyalty and solid performance brought job security. This was mutually beneficial. The executive gained a respectable income and a high degree of security. The company gained loyal, hard-working executives.

This unspoken pact became known as the psychological contract. The originator of the phrase was the social psychologist Ed Schein of MIT. Schein's interest in the employee–employer relationship developed during the late 1950s. Schein noted the similarities between the brainwashing of POWs which he had witnessed during the Korean War and the corporate indoctrination carried out by the likes of GE and IBM. The ability of strong values to influence groups of people is a strand which has continued throughout Schein's work.

As Schein's link with brainwashing suggests, there was more to the psychological contract than a cozy mutually beneficial deal. It raised a number of issues. First, the psychological contract was built around loyalty. 'The most important single contribution required of an executive, certainly the most universal qualification, is loyalty [allowing] domination by the organization personality,' noted Chester Barnard in *The Functions of the Executive* (1938).[81] (The word 'domination' suggests which way Barnard saw the balance of power falling.) While loyalty is a positive quality, it can easily become blind. What if the corporate strategy is wrong or the company is engaged in unlawful or immoral acts? Also, there is the question of loyal to what? Thirty years ago, corporate values were assumed rather than explored.

The second issue raised by the psychological contract was that of perspectives. With careers neatly mapped out, executives were hardly encouraged to look over the corporate parapets to seek out broader viewpoints. The corporation became a self-contained and self-perpetuating world supported by a complex array of checks, systems and hierarchies.

The company was right

The company was right. Customers, who existed in the ethereal world outside the organization, were often regarded as peripheral. In the 1950s, 1960s and 1970s, no executives ever lost their jobs by delivering poor quality or indifferent service. Indeed, in some organizations, executives only lost their jobs by defrauding their employer or insulting their boss. Jobs for life was the refrain and, to a large extent for executives, the reality.

Clearly, such an environment was hardly conducive to the fostering of dynamic risk takers. The psychological contract rewarded the steady foot soldier, the safe pair of hands. It was hardly surprising, therefore, that when Rosabeth Moss Kanter came to examine corporate life for the first time in her 1977 book, *Men and Women of the Corporation*, she found that the central characteristic expected of a manager was 'dependability'.[82]

The psychological contract rewarded the steady foot soldier, the safe pair of hands

The reality was that the psychological contract placed a premium on loyalty rather than ability and allowed a great many poor performers to seek out corporate havens. It was also significant that the psychological contract was regarded as the preserve of management. Lower down the hierarchy, people were hired and fired with abandon.

As the use of the past tense suggests, recent years have seen radical changes to the psychological contract between employers and employees. The rash of downsizing in the 1980s and 1990s marked the end of the psychological contract which had existed for decades.

Expectations have now changed on both sides. Employers no longer wish to make commitments – even implicit ones – to long-term employment. The emphasis is on flexibility. On the other side, employees are keen to develop their skills and take charge of their own careers. Employability is the height of fashion – though as we shall see, it is not universally popular.

As a result, the new psychological contract is more likely to be built on developing skills than blind loyalty. The logic is that if a company invests in an individual's development, the employee will become more loyal. The trouble is that the employee also becomes more employable by other companies.

> The new psychological contract is more likely to be built on developing skills than blind loyalty

In effect the balance has shifted. The original and long-standing psychological contract created an artificial balance based on inefficient behaviour. Its emphasis was on loyalty and reliability rather than performance. Performance was assumed. Downsizing and the decimation of middle management swung the pendulum towards corporations. Managerial job security was overturned. Now, it is employees who potentially hold the balance of power. In the age of flexible employment, downsizing and career management, loyalty is increasingly elusive as managers flit from job to job, company to company.

The old psychological contract, with its inherent safety and clarity, is now being re-evaluated as a corporate nirvana. We never had it so good. The trouble is that the concept of jobs for life was largely a mirage. The grass is always greener. Companies may have been prepared to stick with the same managers throughout their careers, but often the companies themselves didn't last.

(Whether this was due to the inertia of management is open to debate.) Research repeatedly shows that companies don't last very long. One survey of corporate life expectancy in Japan and Europe came up with 12.5 years as the average life expectancy of all firms. London Business School's Arie de Geus estimates that the average life expectancy of a multinational corporation is 40 to 50 years. One-third of 1970's Fortune 500 had disappeared by 1983. Not much security there.

> The new challenge is for both sides to make the psychological contract an explicit arrangement

The ebb and flow of corporate life means that the traditional psychological contract is unlikely to return. But there will always be a psychological contract between employer and employee. In any employment deal, each side carries expectations, aspirations and an understanding – which may be right or wrong – of the expectations and aspirations of the other side. The new challenge is for both sides to make the psychological contract an explicit arrangement.

the richer the better

Just across the River Thames from Britain's bustling commercial centre in the Square Mile is the flagship of hi-fi retailer Richer Sounds. You wouldn't guess it from the outside, but this tiny store, with day-glo stickers plastered on the windows announcing unbeatable prices and the inside piled high with CD players and other sound equipment, is the hottest piece of retail real estate on the planet – and that's official.

At £17,000 per square foot, the store's prolific sales performance merits a regular entry in *The Guinness Book of Records* as the world's busiest retail outlet and makes the typical UK performance for the industry of £650 look decidedly pedestrian. With just 200 employees – or 'colleagues' as co-workers are known – and a turnover of £25 million, the company is a retail phenomenon.

Its success, and that of the other 25 Richer Sounds stores in the UK and Ireland, can be attributed to the radical ideas of founder Julian Richer – a thirty-something-year-old, pony-tailed entrepreneur who has turned British retailing on its head.

Richer opened the London Bridge store in 1978 at the age of 18. Shrewdly located near one of the main railway stations serving the City, it capitalized on passing trade from the thousands of commuters who stream across London

Bridge each day. Noting that manufacturers were constantly releasing new products that were often very similar to existing lines, Richer bought up old stock, offering his customers good old-fashioned value for money. But the real difference was in the service and friendliness of the sales staff. In a sector where lack-lustre service and high staff turnover are the norm, sales people who knew the products inside out and made it their business to give sound advice made a refreshing change. Customers were so impressed they told their friends.

virtual visit **www.richersounds.com**

The company's success has made Richer's business philosophy a much sought-after commodity. Retailing giants including Asda, the supermarket chain, and Sears seek his advice, and Richer has also published a book – *The Richer Way*.[83]

His approach to business can be summed up in a single word: respect. Respect for customers – through exceptional service; and respect for employees – paying a good wage and providing real incentives including a 15 per cent profit share. 'Respect to the individual has always been a guiding principle for me,' Richer says. '"Do as you would be done by" should apply as much at work as in any other area of life.'

At Richer Sounds that means treating all 'colleagues' as if they are part of an extended family. That's why every new employee gets an information pack welcoming them to the business and setting out the company's aims and values.

Aim number one is: 'to provide second-to-none customer service and value for money for our customer'. Number two: 'to provide ourselves with secure well-paid jobs, working in a stimulating equal opportunities environment'. Number three: 'to be profitable to ensure our long-term growth and survival'.

New recruits also get to know their way around Richer's home. Most of their training is done there, in a school and dormitory behind his mansion in Yorkshire. But then, like other true entrepreneurs, he's always been prepared to go against conventional wisdom.

In total disregard for the first rule of retailing, 'location, location, location', for example, most of his outlets are in backstreet sites. What he saves on premises

– rent costs are just 2 per cent of turnover compared with his rivals' 10 per cent – he invests in staff. The reasoning is simple – customers want service not fancy showrooms.

At 29, managing director David Robinson is a 13-year veteran at Richer Sounds. He joined the company at 16. He says: 'What makes us different is that we don't spend money on expensive shop-fittings and locations; we spend it on our employees, motivating them to give excellent customer service.'

But that doesn't mean skimping on the useful stuff. For example, stores offer a variety of novel features: a listening room for customers to check out the equipment in comfort; a review bar which hands out industry reviews of equipment; porter service and traffic warden watch (on Saturdays); free after sales advice; local delivery for disabled customers; free coffee – and ice-pops in the summer. Customers buying sound systems also get an after sales phone call to check they're really happy with their purchase.

In addition, receipts have a form for customers to return saying what they think of the service. Every time a customer ticks excellent that sales assistant receives a £3 bonus – whatever the value of the transaction. It means, for example, that a customer can spend £5, be delighted with the service and the sales person gets £3 – that's 60 per cent of the sale price.

If a customer says service is 'poor', on the other hand, the sales person is fined £3. (The money isn't actually docked from their wages but anyone in the red at the end of the month has some serious explaining to do.) On a Monday morning, staff are told their scores in the last week.

But the incentives don't end there. Every month the three winning stores in the company's customer service competition – the Richer Way League – win a car for a month – and not just any old car. Two get Bentleys and the other a Jaguar XJS convertible. The car is theirs to use as they wish. The company pays for petrol (gas); and even provides a chauffeur for two days if staff don't drive.

Then there's the employee hardship fund. The company pays 1 per cent of all profits into a special fund which provides grants and interest free loans for employees or members of their families falling on hard times. It doesn't dish out money for car loans, but should an employee's partner be made redundant or suffer an accident not covered by insurance, then the fund is there to help.

'The hire and fire attitude has no place in an organization that is serious about customer service,' says Richer: 'Staff won't be loyal to the organization unless it is loyal to them. Training courses and fancy Christmas parties are no substitute for basic trust. Treating your staff better will make your business perform better. It's that simple. It's no good saying you cannot afford to look after your staff: you can't afford not to.'

At Richer Sounds they also have the strange idea that work should be fun. Not only that, but that everyone should do less of it. Workaholics and people who refuse to delegate are frowned upon and anyone caught working six days a week has to answer to Richer himself, who sets an example by working only one week in two.

The company also has five holiday homes around the UK and Ireland, with plans for another in Paris. Any employee, together with their family and friends (and pets), can use them.

'It's first come, first served,' explains David Robinson. If someone hasn't been able to get away all year then they might get preference over a colleague wanting to book a second holiday, but that's only fair. Managers certainly don't get any special treatment.'

Motivation the Richer way is also about involving people in the running of the business. Once a month, staff are given £5 to go to the pub and sit quietly over a drink thinking up ways to improve the business. The employee who comes up with the best suggestion each quarter wins a trip on the Orient Express or a day at Brands Hatch motor racing circuit or a health farm.

The company will even pay half the price of an airline ticket to the USA if employees come back with a side of A4 giving details of how US retailing techniques could be imported.

Staff loyalty, too, is celebrated. There's the 'Five Year Club', for example, where every employee who has been with the company more than five years is invited for an anniversary lunch with Richer at one of London's finest restaurants – the Connaught, the Savoy or the Ritz. There, he says, they enjoy 'a fabulous lunch right through to the brandy and cigars – and a good laugh'.

With five years at the company under her belt, Lol Lecanu is a sales assistant at the London Bridge. She says: 'The difference between Richer Sounds and other retailers is that the company really cares about people. They don't want dumb sales assistants with gold stars on their name badges. If you're encouraged to use your intelligence and independence in dealing with customers then they relate to you as a human being rather than a clone or a robot. The company is successful because it treats customers as individuals. A hi-fi is a major purchase – whether its £200 or £2,000 – you should treat people well when they're spending that sort of money.'

'We always try to go that extra mile,' she adds. 'We'll literally keep the shop open as late as there are customers there. We frequently stay open forty-five minutes or an hour later than closing time if there's someone still in the shop. Or if a customer is having problems setting up their system one of us will go to their home, even if it's 25 miles out of our way. The important thing is that they're happy.'

> Richer Sounds is recognized in its industry as generating more suggestions per employee than any other company

If the company doesn't stock a particular line, that even means recommending competitors. One customer who came into the store recently, for example, was surprised when Lol told him that even though Richer Sounds didn't stock the speakers he wanted, she'd help him find them.

'He was dead set on these particular speakers,' she explains, 'so I picked up the phone and called round our competitors all over the country to find some he could listen to. He was pretty surprised, but not as surprised as the sales people on the other end of the line when I told them who I was and why I was calling.'

Richer Sounds is recognized in its industry as generating more suggestions per employee than any other company. Says Lol: 'We have suggestions meetings where the company gives each colleague £5 to go down the pub. We have a few jars and think about how we might improve the way we do things or make customers more comfortable. The ideas don't have to be cost-saving; in fact most of the best ones aren't.'

Colleague suggestions which have been adopted include: providing tape measures so that customers can measure equipment to see if it fits the dimensions of their room or furniture; comfortable chairs; coffee machines; mail order catalogues; providing lollies and candy; a special handle to help carry purchases more easily; ensuring all systems have the necessary leads and plugs included; and even providing black plastic bin liners so that potential burglars won't see what customers are carrying into their homes.

> The Richer message is a simple one: keeping costs down and customers and staff happy makes a successful business

In an industry where staff are frequently moving, the company has a very low labour turnover; shrinkage too – the retail euphemism for theft – is much lower than the norm; and the rate of absenteeism is between 1 and 2 per cent compared with a UK average of 4 to 5 per cent

Staff from support departments such as accounts and marketing also spend time in the stores so they understand the problems – and they are included in incentive schemes. Directors, too, have to spend at least one week a year working on the shop floor, and in the run-up to Christmas Richer spends a day working in each of the 25 outlets.

The Richer message is a simple one: keeping costs down and customers and staff happy makes a successful business. If you get these basics right then profits pretty much take care of themselves. As Julian Richer puts it: 'Profits are simply an indicator that staff are happy and you are getting the customer service right.'

taking control

C areer management is a new phenomenon. As we have seen, in the distant past life unrolled before you. It was largely not yours to control. Then, during the twentieth century, the corporation emerged as the determiner of careers. Now, careers have to be increasingly managed by individuals. It is we, as individuals, who make the choices and call the shots.

> Happiness comes from working at what we are good at and in ways that suit our abilities. The trouble is that this rarely happens

The objective, Peter Drucker has observed, is simple enough. Happiness comes from working at what we are good at and in ways that suit our abilities. The trouble is that this rarely happens. The reason, says Drucker, is because we often have little idea of what we are good at. We should ask: What are my strengths? How do I perform? What are my values? Where do I belong? What should my contribution be?

The route to outstanding performance is to identify and improve your unique skills and then to find jobs or assignments which match your skills, values, etc. Ask questions, find the

> Gen e have started asking the right questions. Some have found the answers

answers, and then you are equipped to make the right decisions for your career – and life – development. Gen e have started asking the right questions. Some have found the answers.

In typically breathless style, management guru Tom Peters ushers in a new era in the world of gen e careers. 'Regardless of age, regardless of position, regardless of the business we happen to be in, all of us need to understand the importance of branding,' says Peters. 'We are CEOs of our own companies: Me Inc. To be in business today, our most important job is to be head marketer for the brand called You.'[84]

Peters argues that Marlboro Friday in 1993 (when Philip Morris slashed the prices of its premium cigarette brand) marked the end of a generation of big brands. The new world of brands is radically different. The big names still exist but they no longer have a monopoly over the art of branding. Peters points to the rise of the internet as evidence of a new, more personal brand generation. After all, you return to the website you trust and gain the most value from. Increasingly we need to promote our own personal brands through such things as developing our contacts or updating our CVs. Self-creation is the order of the day.

Peters even provides a personal brand equity evaluation to help you on your way. 'If you're really smart, you figure out what it takes to create a distinctive role for yourself – you create a message and a strategy to promote the brand called You,' says Peters. (What is interesting – and paradoxical – is that amid this branding frenzy, Peters' idea of what constitutes a brand remains somewhat traditional. 'The brand is a promise of the value you'll receive,' he says: a definition as applicable to a pack of cornflakes as to an interesting CV.)

> **Self-creation is the order of the day**

Resumés rule. Bagel queen Danielle Downing took the scenic route. From the time she received her MBA from the Wharton School, University of Pennsylvania, it took Downing eight years to turn her business dream – Bagel Street – into a reality. 'When I was doing my MBA at Wharton in the early 1990s, people weren't really thinking about starting their own business,' she observes. 'But now, a lot of the students there want to do an internet start-up as soon as they leave.'[85]

> **Resumés rule**

The tide has turned. They want to be closer to the action. They want to call the shots. They want to be entrepreneurial. They want to challenge the business establishment. 'Over the past three or four years there's been a drift away from the mainstream recruiters in the US, and we're beginning to see the same trend over here,' says Lesley Aylward, director of London Business School's careers centre.[86]

Research carried out in 1999 provides one of the earliest indications of how this new generation of high-fliers think about their careers. Spanning more than seventy countries, it represents the first serious attempt to identify the career culture of the highly educated and internationally mobile cadre of managers who will be the business leaders of tomorrow.

Sponsored by the Career Innovation Research Group – an alliance of eight multinational employers, including British Aerospace, PricewaterhouseCoopers, Reuters, Cap Gemini and SmithKline Beecham – formed in response (perhaps belatedly) to the worldwide shortage of talented young professionals, *Riding the Wave* documents the findings of an internet survey among 1,000 international managers (average age 29) and a series of international seminars carried out between June 1998 and April 1999.[87] It provides important insights into the way this new generation of high-fliers view career and work related issues. The initiative targeted the next generation of business leaders. All participants had first degrees, and the majority (68 per cent) had higher degrees. Just under a third of them had an MBA.

Coordinated by Whiteway Research International Limited, the research covered 73 nations from Europe, North and South America, Africa, Asia and Australasia. The largest representations were from the USA (11 per cent) and the UK (8 per cent).

The calibre of the managers participating in the survey underlines the increasing importance attached to staff retention. It will make uncomfortable reading for employers still clinging to traditional approaches to career management.

The findings suggest that today's international high-fliers have a short career horizon. On average they plan to stay with their current employer just three years – although only 8 per cent completely ruled out 'staying for the long term'.

Despite their short-term career intentions, these young professionals still express loyalty to their managers, clients and organizations. However, their greatest commitment is to their immediate colleagues and staff. They describe their top three 'career values' as wide horizons; work–life balance; and professional expertise. They see wide horizons as maximizing future options, meeting new people and having new and different experiences.

Significantly, stability comes bottom of the list of their career values. Instead, these high-fliers rely more on their employability – their ability to keep their career options open and maximize their personal and professional development – to ensure future success.

The majority of these future leaders appear to have a strong psychological contract – a perfomance contract – with their employers. But most are searching for a 'development contract'. Edouard de Lamarzelle, general manager of Volvo Insurance (a subsidiary of Volvo) in France, is typical of the new breed of gen e high-flier who took part in the survey. Personal career development is the big issue for them. 'I sometimes compare myself to a stock that is quoted on a market,' he observes. 'It means that I realize I have to be valuable, and the more valuable I am, the higher the position and the package will be.'

'The new business environment (mergers, acquisitions, etc.) makes us think "external" and not "internal", i.e. to position oneself within an industry sector instead of the company only. In other words, I have to be as valuable to my boss as to my competitors,' said another.

That includes international experience at a young age. Over two-thirds of those surveyed saw an international assignment as important for their future career development. And almost two-fifths would be prepared to live and work abroad for more than five years.

'Our environment is naturally international,' says Edouard de Lamarzelle. 'We increase our options if we speak several languages and our goals do not change whether we work in NYC, Paris, London or Singapore; it has to be an experience that enhances our value.'

Gen e are more mobile than previous generations. Once seen as a serious obstacle, the trailing spouse issue – managers being less willing to move because of the effect of the upheaval on their partners – does not appear to be as significant as for previous generations. Almost half of those with a partner (48 per cent) and 46 per cent of those with children reported that their mobility is not constrained.

Many of the young high-fliers also recognize the importance of entrepreneurial experience. Many listed business start-ups among their alternative career options. Other popular alternatives included working in the voluntary sector, non-government organizations and, in particular, the United Nations. Gen e have a different agenda to their ancestors corporate man and the baby boomers.

The changing attitudes of high-fliers create new challenges for employers – a point acknowledged by Carolyn Nimmy of Cap Gemini Group, a founder member of Career Innovation Research Group. 'In the past, many workers had the expectation that the company was largely responsible for their careers,' she notes. 'Today, the

> Gen e have a different agenda to their ancestors corporate man and the baby boomers

sentiment among young workers is one of career ownership, or of being the master of one's own destiny. These young professionals are very comfortable and confident in managing their careers and pushing for the next wave or challenge. They are not prepared to wait their turn or do their time. The companies that succeed in this environment will be those that can recognize this change and respond by offering challenges and development opportunities quickly and constantly – providing rewards not based on tenure, but on merit.'

The report's authors, Jonathan Winter and Dr Charles Jackson, make a number of recommendations for employers. In particular, they suggest that companies should openly negotiate new career partnerships, with each person or group, to create realistic expectations on both sides.

Greater flexibility, they say, will make it possible to accommodate changing career needs. That would involve a shift in thinking by employers away from the traditional relationship with employees, to a looser arrangement which included keeping in touch and tracking. This would more closely resemble the alumni network relationship that universities, especially business schools, have with former students: 'They may be full-time, part-time, or even consultants. Others will be on a career break but still connected.'

For gen e MBAs, there is no career downside. Experience of a failed start-up is no longer seen as a blot on the CV. In fact, the reverse is true. Blue chip companies are desperately seeking entrepreneurial elan. This is a boon to the new entrepreneurs. When Danielle Downing took her MBA at Wharton, things were different. 'The graduating class of '91 at Wharton had 50 per cent unemployment. It was bad. Fifty per cent of graduates couldn't get a job. Now the consulting firms and the investment banks are madly courting MBA students. They're worried because the new MBAs all want to set up internet businesses. It's wild.'

'For the students it's a win:win. They know they can go out and have a go with a .com business and it won't hurt them. They think "If it works out great, I'll make a load of money." If not, they're trained in the internet industry. They can get an even better job with an investment bank in two or three years' time – and get a premium for their experience. They'll be more marketable. They'll be experts in internet start-ups. Investment banks will jump at the chance to employ them. It's really wild right now.'

> It's infectious. Previously stalwart corporate citizens are jumping ship to join the revolution

For these new entrepreneurs the notion of job security is immaterial. 'You have to want to take risks and really believe in your product or service,' says Downing. 'The other thing is you have to want to do it without a corporate structure. You have to want to do it without any safety net.'

This creates a problem for traditional companies, which increasingly have to create entrepreneurial opportunities within – including stock options – to tempt talent. In future, that may not be enough to stop the charge of the entrepreneurs. It's infectious. Previously stalwart corporate citizens are jumping ship to join the revolution. Young or old, the desire to flex their entrepreneurial muscles is more than they can bear. Jan Leschley, chief executive of SmithKline Beecham, has been bitten by the internet bug. Famed for the size of his remuneration package, he cannot wait to leave SB and get digging for internet gold. He's probably not motivated by the money, but by the excitement of being involved in something radical, something new and challenging. As he says: 'If you don't operate in internet time you can just forget the whole thing.'

This is now causing a major drain on big companies. Even Microsoft, once lauded as an exemplar of staff retention, has seen a steady trickle of key staff leaving to start their own businesses. When the CEO of Andersen Consulting decides to up sticks and go – as George Shaheen did when he quit to join the Webvan Group, an online grocery delivery company – you know something has changed.

'A career is a line of work. You can say that your career is to be a lawyer or a securities analyst – but usually it's not the same thing as your calling. You can have different careers at different points in your life,' says Timothy Butler, director of MBA career development programmes at Harvard Business School.[88]

> This is gen e's attitude to working life: a pageant of careers

This is gen e's attitude to working life: a pageant of careers, a variety of interesting and fulfilling strands which pull apart and come together as their careers unfold.

Figure 38.1 | Learning to blur

In their book *BLUR: The Speed of Change in the Connected Economy*, Stan Davis and Christopher Meyer suggest that three factors – speed, intangibles and connectivity – are changing the face of business in the post-internet economy.[89]

The only answer, they say, is to BLUR your business. Along with 50 ways to BLUR your business, the two offer 10 tips on how to BLUR yourself:

1 Blur the divide between work life and life: everyone knows the line is already indistinct; stop trying to keep the two separate. Run your home like you run your office.

2 Have your cake and eat it, too: in the BLUR economy knowledge is King; the more you give away the more you'll get back.

3 Seek novelty forever: skills wear out quickly in the new economy; don't get stuck in a rut.

4 Moonlight from strength: people used to work two jobs when they needed extra money. Now you can moonlight for the fun of it.

5 Sell your value on the Web: the Web is a great leveller. It gives you and the giant corporation an equal shot at the global market. Use that power.

6 Let the market, not the company determine your worth: don't wait to be promoted, use the marketplace to evaluate your value.

7 Become a free agent while still on the payroll: don't think of yourself as a wage slave, think of yourself as self-employed on someone's pay-roll. It frees the mind.

8 Brand yourself: writers talk about finding their distinctive voice; you too need to find your special groove.

9 Securitize yourself: pop star David Bowie has sold shares in his future earnings; you can do the same.

10 Manage your new dual career: we all have two careers now – one inside the company and the other in the marketplace. You need to manage both.

the trouble with employability

What have companies come up with to replace the old career ladder? Not much. Much beloved of human resources professionals, the concept of employability is meant to provide the basis for a new psychological contract between workers and employers. With companies no longer able to guarantee long-term job security for employees, employability represents a shift to a new deal whereby employers offer shorter job tenure with an undertaking to provide skills development and training which will make staff more employable later.

> Today, loyalty can no longer be taken for granted – on either side

Employability grew out of the delayering and downsizing exercises that occurred at the end of the 1980s and in the early 1990s. The bond of trust between employee and employer was irredeemably broken.

In the face of change, HR departments were forced to rethink what the company was able to offer in return for a degree of loyalty. The new message from organizations is that 'we can't offer you a job for life, but we will add to your employability'. Typically, this involves a move away from the traditional parternalistic approach to career development towards one where the employee is expected to manage his or her own career prospects. Today, loyalty can no longer be taken for granted – on either side. Employability is an attempt by organizations to provide a new basis for trust in the future. As management commentator Charles Handy notes in his book *The Hungry Spirit*: 'The psychological contract between employers and employed has changed … No longer can anyone expect to be able to hand over their lives to an organization.'[90]

Whether employability is more than simply a conceptual underpinning for the reality of modern working arrangements, however, remains to be seen. Some commentators argue that the next step down this road is to move to explicit employability contracts. This would involve replacing traditional employment contracts, based on ongoing employment, with renewable fixed term contracts whereby employees negotiate pay and development opportunities on an individual basis.

But not everyone buys into employability as a concept. One of the most vociferous critics is the influential business commentator Richard Pascale, formerly of Stanford Business School. 'A new social contract based on "employability" is the sound of one hand clapping,' he has observed. 'Its impetus is wishful thinking masquerading as a concept – a lived happily ever after ending to replace the broken psychological contract of the past. The hard truth is, there is no painless remedy. In fact, the death of job security, like any death, means that we have to learn to relate to the pain, not escape from it.'[91]

> Not everyone buys into employability as a concept

Pascale sees employability as an inadequate response. 'Once upon a time, corporations were like ocean liners,' he says. 'Anyone fortunate enough to secure a berth cruised through a career and disembarked at retirement age. A clear agreement charted the voyage: in return for loyalty, sacrifice, bureaucratic aggravation, and the occasional demanding boss, you received job security for life. In theory, employability aims to restore the quid pro quo between the ocean liner and its crew. Instead of a lifelong voyage, companies take smaller excursions with crew members who understand that they might change boats after any trip. In exchange for employees making dedicated efforts during these shorter engagements, the company agrees to pay somewhat higher

> Instead of a lifelong voyage, companies take smaller excursions with crew members who understand that they might change boats after any trip

wages and to invest in the employees' development. This makes them more marketable when it comes time to move on.'

But as he points out, it's not that easy. Employability is a simplistic attempt to repair rents in the social fabric. 'There is a fundamental flaw with this convenient new arrangement: philosophically, employability is a slick palliative that sidesteps the need to confront our essential humanness.' There are, he says, three interlocking elements to the problem. First, job loss and employment insecurity are an inherently painful experience that triggers a loss of self-esteem and social identity. Second, corporations and those who work for them cannot resolve these issues by themselves. Third, a new social context is needed to legitimize and deal with the grief associated with the experiences of loss and betrayal in our working lives.

It is too early to tell whether employability is more than a corporate convenience. Along with empowerment, it may turn out to be something of a Pandora's box. Having opened the lid on the loyalty issue, most companies have yet to fully come to terms with the wider implications. (We look at the entire issue of loyalty later.) In the coming years, with skills shortages predicted, they are likely to reap the whirlwind. Smart employees will master the new rules of the employment game and may hold them to ransom at a later date. Having made it abundantly clear that they are prepared to dump employees when times are tough, organizations shouldn't be at all surprised if the most talented employees feel no sense of loyalty to them when times are good.

A 1999 report by the Institute of Employment Studies[92] notes: 'Employability is a concept that has joined the mainstream of individual human resources and national policy vocabulary. It has been summoned as the means by which individuals can cope with changing employment conditions, organizations can maintain their ability to adapt and succeed and the nation can enhance its competitiveness. However, despite such grand hopes, pinning down the concept can be elusive and turning the rhetoric into anything that can serve as a firm basis for action can be frustrating.'

corporate life and death

e inc.

The modern corporation is under siege. Until now, the corporation has been able to maintain its powerful status in society through the management of information inside and outside its borders. When it came to its employees, the activist groups and the media generally, the corporation could maintain and perhaps gain influence in key areas (marketplace; factory floor; AGMs) through priority access to information.

> The modern corporation is under siege

'The corporate advantage lay in the ability to source and disseminate (where *appropriate*) information more quickly and more accurately than its foes. But what is the impact on the power relations if the humble individual can get hold of this information with equal speed and ease?' asks Gerry Griffin in *The Power Game*.[93] 'In many respects, the modern technological age poses a greater threat to corporate power than those other antagonists such as the activist groups – because the threat is amorphous. The threat poses a challenge not only for the corporation but also for other previously fixed institutions of power such as the church and government. In the new age, the ways in which third party bodies or institutions represent the interests of the individual are changing radically and will continue to do so.'

virtual visit   www.thepowergame.com

With their power being questioned and often eroded, the world's corporations face big questions from gen e:

- How do they harness the power of their employees?
- How do they ensure that their employees can fulfil their goals, be true to their own personal beliefs and yet act in the interests of the company they work for?
- How do they forge a bond of trust, a partnership with their employees to bind the employee to the company?
- How does the company find common ground with its employees?

Corporations ain't what they used to be – they can't be

If corporations are to provide some answers – and there is precious little evidence that big companies can do so – they need to structure themselves differently and manage their activities in radically different ways with new priorities.

Corporations ain't what they used to be – they can't be.

Look at the creative melting pot of IDEO. So potent have IDEO's creative juices proved that *Fortune* magazine described the company's seemingly chaotic design studio as 'one of Silicon Valley's secret weapons'. The secret of its own success, the industrial design firm believes, lies in its ability to sustain a culture of innovation.

Others think so, too. With the words of management guru Tom Peters no doubt ringing in its ears ('innovate or die'), in recent years IDEO has become a magnet

virtual visit   www.ideo.com

for multinationals which believe that rubbing shoulders with the consultancy will make their own company cultures more innovative. It's a formula that seems to work.

IDEO is the largest industrial product design firm in the world. It has been involved in such diverse projects as helping create the very first Apple Computer mouse and the design of the 25-foot mechanical whale in the 'Free Willy' films. Its business is innovation – something that is very much in demand at present.

The UK office traces its origins back to 1969 when Bill Moggridge founded a design firm in London. Later, he opened another office in Silicon Valley. In 1991

Moggridge merged his businesses with two other leading design firms in the region: Matrix Product Design, run by Mike Nuttall, and David Kelley Design. IDEO was born.

Today, the company has a turnover of around $50 million. With offices in Palo Alto, San Francisco, Boston, Grand Rapids, New York, Milan, Tel Aviv, Tokyo and London it employs a total 350 staff. In recent years, it has worked on projects for the likes of Xerox, Motorola, British Airways, Black and Decker, Hewlett-Packard, Nike and Shell.

But others want to get even closer. Companies hoping to catch the innovation bug include the Korean electronics conglomerate Samsung, which has created a joint design laboratory with IDEO in Palo Alto, California, and Steelcase, the US office furniture company which has taken an equity holding. Both hope to learn the secrets of sustaining an innovation culture.

So how do IDEO do it? European director Tim Brown, one of 45 staff based in Camden Town in London, has some unsettling news for those who like their work spaces tidy. 'Above all else,' he insists, 'innovation requires a willingness to embrace chaos. It means giving rein to people who are opinionated, willfull and delight in challenging the rules. It demands a loose management structure that does not isolate people in departments or on the rungs of a ladder. It needs flexible work spaces that encourage a cross-fertilization of ideas. And it requires risk-taking.'

> 'Innovation requires a willingness to embrace chaos'

Tom Peters agrees. 'IDEO is a zoo,' he wrote after a recent visit to the company's Palo Alto office. 'Experts of all flavors co-mingle in "offices" that look more like cacophonous kindergarten classrooms.' In Peters-speak that's a serious compliment.

Despite intense pressure and tight deadlines, the company maintains an air of creative anarchy which it believes is the ultimate innovation environment. Staff are encouraged to 'play' at work, and the most important rule is to break the rules. IDEO deliberately employs an eclectic group which includes cognitive psychologists and computer scientists as well as industrial designers. Between them they create around 90 new products a year.

Along with the last word in computer imaging, IDEO offices are literally strewn with cardboard, foam, wood and plastic prototypes. Staff work wherever they happen to be and scribbled notes are scattered all around. To the untrained eye it may look like a chaotic mess, but David Kelley, the company's 46-year-old founder and front man, describes the firm as 'a living laboratory of the workplace'. 'The company is in a state of perpetual experimentation,' he said. 'We're constantly trying new ideas in our projects, our work space, even our culture.'

The company epitomizes the project-based organization. All work is organized into project teams which form and disband in a matter of weeks or months. There are no permanent job assignments or job titles. 'If a client wants to know what someone's job title is, we'll give them a job title. But people change their roles so often and wear so many different hats that job titles are fairly meaningless,' explains Rosemary Lees, in the London office.

IDEO also believes that designers, in particular, benefit from seeing the work and cultures in other offices for themselves. Staff go on six-month secondments to other offices – and are also free to transfer themselves to another location if they can find a colleague prepared to switch.

But it is the company's special approach to brainstorming which has attracted the attention of other firms. These sessions have been elevated almost to the status of a science.

Typically, project leaders call a brainstorming session at the start of a new assignment. People are invited to attend and most sessions involve a multi-disciplinary group of around eight participants. (Attendance is voluntary, but refusal to take part is frowned upon.)

Once the brainstorming starts, participants can doodle or scribble on almost anything – there are whiteboards on the walls, and conference tables are covered in white paper. Low tech is accompanied by high tech in the form of multimedia presentations using video and computer projections.

To ensure the best results, the firm's five principles of brainstorming are displayed on the walls: Stay focused on the topic. Encourage wild ideas. Defer judgement. Build on the ideas of others. One conversation at a time.

The aim is to create a whirlwind of activity and ideas. Speed is essential to the process, with the most promising ideas being developed and worked up into prototypes in just a few days. To make brainstorming more effective, the company has also developed a special type of camera copier which photographs whatever drawing and scribblings emerge from the sessions.

But even the firm's brainstorming rules need challenging. According to Tim Brown, there is a danger in formalizing any aspect of the innovative process. 'Having a process is useful,' he says, 'but it's a delicate balance between process and innovation. You have to be very careful that you don't end up with a system that squeezes out the innovation. It's no good if you crank the handle and you know exactly what is going to come out the other end. You also have to be prepared to fail a lot. The great thing about a prototype culture like ours is that we have lots of spectacular failures. We celebrate that.'

You don't have to be in a wacky creative business to embrace the gen e buzz of change and then change some more. Take Pearl Assurance, a life insurance company. At one time, Pearl looked all but doomed. A poor regulation compliance record meant the PIA, the pensions watchdog, was within a whisker of closing the company down; and 16 consecutive months of falling market share had made its commercial position precarious.

Today, the picture looks very different. During 1997 alone, Pearl, part of the Australian group AMP, reported a 46 per cent increase in sales over the previous year. Over the same period, staff turnover, a key indicator of the mood of an organization, dropped from 28 per cent to just 12 per cent.

Pearl's comeback stems from a radical overhaul of its management culture. A new chief executive seems to have helped. Richard Surface, the new managing director, was brought in from Sun Life in 1995. Insiders at the company say the American's dynamic style was just what was needed to dispel the 'complacent' attitude at the top. Since his arrival, Surface has replaced about two-thirds of the senior management team, taking a new broom to what was an outdated and hierarchical management structure.

> You don't have to be in a wacky creative business to embrace the gen e buzz of change and then change some more

His enthusiasm for change proved too much for the management consultants McKinsey and Co. The strategy experts were brought in to advise on the best way to implement change. They favoured a cautious, softly, softly approach to restructuring. But Surface felt the patient needed more urgent surgery. 'Pearl did not have the luxury of time on our side,' he said. 'The best of the sales force were leaving, the worst were hanging around; productivity was dropping and we were selling uneconomically.' He felt that speed was of the essence, so 'people got through the pain to see the gain'.

The men from McKinsey were overruled and a radical overhaul of management embarked upon. Costs were slashed and the product range halved. Twelve out of fourteen of the top management team were replaced, with four outsiders brought in to give a broader perspective. The sales force was also overhauled. Terry Shrimpton joined the company from the Prudential, restructuring the sales force. Instead of a single agent covering a small territory, the company widened the catchment area and introduced teams of three – two agents and an area manager. More than 1,000 jobs were lost in the process.

Much of the credit for the volte-face, however, has to go to the remaining staff at Pearl, who have responded magnificently to a series of change initiatives. These include a new training strategy and the introduction of new working practices. 'Better by Miles' is a training campaign introduced to make staff at Pearl more responsive to customers. Designed by the specialist training consultancy Oxford Training, it involves a series of one- and two-day development modules to help staff make the transition from an old-fashioned insurance firm to a customer-driven service provider. In all, more than 2,500 employees at the company's Peterborough headquarters (about a third of its total workforce) will benefit from the training initiative.

virtual visit   www.pearl.co.uk

'There's much more awareness now of customer needs,' says Pearl's Helen Askey, the training manager responsible for the 'Better by Miles' programme. 'Staff are much more focused on the needs of individual customers, too, rather than treating all customers the same. People are willing to speak up if they see something wrong. Before, there was almost a fear culture here.'

Pearl has also invested in the latest in workplace design, with a series of themed meeting rooms which give employees in the back office a taste of the domestic environments in which sales staff meet their customers. The company has also injected new working practices into what was once a bastion of conservative attitudes. The office makeover includes the Living Room – a mock-up of home, complete with armchairs and coffee table; and the Garden Room with astroturf and picnic tables (next to the Living Room through some patio doors).

For impromptu meetings, there is also the Fast Meeting Room, which staff don't have to book in advance, painted bright yellow to discourage sloth. A stopwatch on the wall inspires users to optimize efficiency with 30-second meetings.

Other innovations include the introduction of flexible work practices. Employees and most managers no longer have designated desks or offices, but are free to sit at any available workspace when they arrive in the morning. 'We call it "romping",' says training manager Helen Askey. 'It's like "hot-desking", but more fun.'

organizational glue

There is no mystery to the stories of organizational transformation. According to Robert Reich, twenty-first century companies will be held together by a new type of 'social glue'. He cites examples from Silicon Valley, where rapidly growing software firms have been able to retain talented individuals by redefining working relationships with the organization.[94] The people these companies rely on could easily go elsewhere. They stay because the firm offers them a good environment to work in and a real sense of community. 'To call these workers "employees"', he says, 'misses the point. They're all shareholders. They're all managers. They're all partners.'

In future, this will be key to creating both a winning business and a humane workplace. 'It's a seller's market for talent,' notes Reich. 'People with the right combination of savvy and ambition can afford to shop for the right boss, the right colleagues, and the right environment. In the old economy, it was a buyer's market: companies had their pick of the crop, and the question they asked was: "Why hire?" Now the question is "Why join up?"'

'Now the question is "Why join up?"'

The answer, Reich claims, is likely to be because the social glue is strong enough to make them want to stick around. Successful companies in future will be those that offer a new model for working relationships based on collaboration and mutual value.

According to Reich, there are six characteristics of these new sorts of working communities:

1 Money makes it mutual: Today's talented workers demand a vested interest. They are looking for stock options as well as salary.

2 Mission makes a difference: Workers want to be part of something that confers meaning onto them and their lives.

3 Learning makes you grow: In the knowledge-based economy, the new coin of the realm is learning. Individuals want to join organizations that give them opportunities to keep on learning.

4 Fun makes it fresh: When people work hard, they need to have fun as well.

5 Pride makes it special: We all like to be affiliated with an organization that feeds our sense of pride.

6 Balance makes it sustainable: The best companies lure talented employees by offering a balance between work and home.

None of this is rocket science. Nor is it wishful thinking. Some companies get it, few more vividly than the software company SAS Institute.

SAS's initiatives are many and varied. It has social glue in sticky abundance. Its base in North Carolina includes a large gym (large enough for two basketball courts), a health clinic and day-care facilities. Other benefits include M&Ms distributed every week (employees may not like them, but it is something journalists always write about), massages, family benefits, a 35-hour week, live music in the canteen, and so on.

As you would expect if you had read motivational theorists from Douglas McGregor to Rosabeth Moss Kanter, SAS is hugely successful – its 1997 sales were $750 million. More to the point, in an age in which corporate loyalty is rare, SAS has a staff turnover rate of 3.7 per cent. (The figure is not an aberration – it has never exceeded 5 per cent.) As a result, it makes massive savings in recruitment and training costs – enough to pay for an awful lot of massages.

'SAS places enormous emphasis on three things: employees, customers, and products,' says Charles Fishman, writing in *Fast Company*.[95] 'Employees and customers, for instance, are surveyed every year. The company says that 80 per cent of the suggestions for product improvements that customers make most frequently eventually find their way into the software. SAS ploughs 30 per cent or more of its revenue (that's revenue, not profit) back into R&D – a higher proportion than any other software company of its size.' The message is that good business can be good for you and can be extraordinarily simple.

> The message is that good business can be good for you and can be extraordinarily simple

Indeed, keeping it simple and humane is the fundamental route to corporate longevity. 'The natural average lifespan of a corporation should be as long as two or three centuries,' writes Arie de Geus in *The Living Company*,[96] noting a few prospering relics such as the Sumitomo Group and the Scandinavian company Stora. Such endemic failure is attributed by de Geus to the focus of managers on profits and the bottom line rather than on the human community which makes up their organization.

In an attempt to get to the bottom of this mystery, de Geus and a number of his Shell colleagues carried out some research to identify the characteristics of corporate longevity. As you would expect, the onus is on keeping excitement to a minimum. More Ronald Reagan than James Dean. The average human centenarian advocates a life of abstinence, caution and moderation, and so it is with companies. The Royal Dutch/Shell team identified four key characteristics. The long-lived were

> Great companies are true to the values of gen e

'sensitive to their environment'; 'cohesive, with a strong sense of identity'; 'tolerant'; and 'conservative in financing' – conclusions echoed in Jerry Porras' and James Collins' *Built to Last*.[97]

These qualities are, perhaps, best interpreted as the bottom line. Great companies are also imaginative and innovative. Great companies are true to the values of gen e.

One company we found that truly epitomizes gen e is the Danish hearing aid company Oticon. Under the guidance of its remarkable president, Lars Kolind, the company has been in the vanguard of management and workplace innovation for more than a decade. 'I was inspired by frustrations in former jobs,' says Kolind, looking back. 'Management seldom made a positive contribution to the development of the business. Too much control: too little spirit, joy and inspiration.'

Oticon, part of the William Demant Group, is probably best known outside Denmark for its pioneering development of the paperless office. During Kolind's time at the helm, the company has made an extraordinary voyage of discovery. (Kolind has now been succeeded by Niels Jacobsen.)

The Oticon story starts like that of many manufacturing companies. Founded in 1904, it was the first hearing instrument company in the world. By the 1970s, it was the number one manufacturer of behind-the-ear hearing aids in the world. But by 1974, its market share began declining as people started using in-the-ear models. By 1987, it had dropped from 15 to 7 per cent and the company was starting to lose money.

Enter Kolind. A former management consultant, he had worked as an associate professor at Copenhagen University, been assistant director of Denmark's National Research Laboratory, and joined Oticon from the private sector at Radiometer AS, a manufacturer of medical instrumentation systems.

His first move was a classic cost-cutting exercise aimed at stripping out the fat that had attached itself to the company in more prosperous times. He pared the company down, shedding staff and raising efficiency. He refocused the business on its key markets. By 1989, the medicine seemed to be working and Oticon returned to profit. But Kolind knew that the changes were not enough. 'It was clear that we could not survive over the next five years without taking a radical step,' he remembers. 'Where was our competitive edge? Nowhere.'

On New Year's Day 1990, he produced his manifesto for change: it was to be nothing short of a revolution. In future, he believed a company's success would be increasingly reliant upon creating the right working environment – one where employees behaved as individuals rather than part of a large organization. Formal organizational structures and hierarchies, he felt, stifled innovation and initiative. They had to go. The question was how to liberate individuals from the corporate fetters. Kolind's answer – deconstruct the organization.

He launched the 300 Project, so called because it aimed to increase productivity at the company's Copenhagen headquarters by 300 per cent over three years. He hoped it would trigger a breakthrough in creativity and innovation.

First, however, the company's structure and working practices had to change. Kolind created a new organizational model based on the idea of replacing permanent departments with a chaotic network of continuously changing project teams. The Spaghetti Organization was born.

Any individual who comes up with a good idea is free to assemble a team and act as project leader. Each project, however, then has to compete with all the other projects trying to get off the ground at any time. In true Darwinian fashion, an employee must attract sufficient resources and support for his or her project or it will perish.

At times, there are up to 100 projects on the go, forming and disbanding as tasks are started or completed. Individuals invariably contribute to more than one project at a time.

Key to freeing up the way people think and work is Oticon's mobile office system. Employees carry their office with them wherever they go at Oticon's headquarters. Desks are not allocated; instead workers use the nearest available workstation, rolling their personal 'Rullemaries' – Rolling Marys or mobile carts – around the hardwood floor to wherever they need to be in the building.

Each mobile cart holds up to thirty hanging folders and other office paraphernalia. The caddy is mounted on wheels and trundled around the office as the employee travels from team to team throughout the day.

Then there's the paperless office concept for which the company is well known. Paper is all but outlawed from the organization. Incoming mail is scanned into the company's computer system before being shredded. Some important documents – legal documents and reports, for example – may be kept for a few days or longer, but the bulk of paper is shredded within hours of arriving.

The shredder is connected to a transparent chute which passes through the company cafeteria directly below, allowing workers on breaks to watch a satis-

virtual visit   www.oticon.com

fying stream of falling paper on its way to the recycling bins. Kolind estimates that the new way of working has reduced circulating paperwork by 80 per cent.

The new way of working seems to work. During the recession of the early 1990s, the company's industry experienced some of the toughest trading conditions in its history. During those dark days, however, Oticon proved the exception to the rule. In 1995, it published figures showing revenues of $160 million and operating profits of $20 million – an increase of 100 per cent on revenue and a tenfold increase in profits on the figures for 1990. At that point many observers thought the revolution had gone far enough, but not Kolind.

By the end of 1995, he sensed that something wasn't right. It had been a hard year, with the company almost exclusively focused on developing and releasing a new line of digital hearing aids. The new products epitomized the breakthrough culture. The problem was that the temporary teams created to push them through had assumed an air of permanence.

'To keep a company alive, one of the jobs of top management is to keep it disorganized'

The disorganized company was becoming dangerously organized. Kolind's solution was to 'explode Oticon in a new direction'. Projects were rearranged geographically within the building. He described the result as 'total chaos' – precisely what he was looking for. As he says: 'To keep a company alive, one of the jobs of top management is to keep it disorganized.'

Kolind left the company but believes the revolution can go on without him. 'I quit Oticon now because I feel that both the company and I will benefit from a change. There is a whole new generation of young people who are ready to run with the ball and why shouldn't I let them do it?'

the loyalty factor

Whatever your view of the organizational future, key to long-term organizational success is some degree of loyalty. But, according to the fashionable pundits and some research, corporate loyalty is dead. Today's employees are loyal to no-one but themselves.

Typically, research by the outplacement consultancy Sanders and Sidney suggests that current working practices have all but destroyed employee loyalty towards their employers.[98] It also highlights a disturbing lack of awareness among companies about the scale of the loss. Over 90 per cent of employees said the loyalty they felt to their employer had decreased, with two-thirds of them reporting that it had 'decreased a lot'. The strength of feeling was consistent across the board, at all levels in organizations and in all age brackets.

Many companies, however, appear to be unaware that employees feel so strongly. The survey indicates a serious mismatch between the way HR departments and employees view the issue. Some 75 per cent of HR professionals interviewed, for example, believe loyalty to the company has decreased only a little or not at all; and fewer than 25 per cent believe it has decreased a lot.

Moreover, those that recognize it as an issue put it down to the wrong reasons. Many HR departments blame the fall in loyalty on external circumstances such as changes in the competitive environment rather than recognizing that it is partly the fault of management for the way it communicates with and treats employees.

Comments Professor David Guest, head of the department of organizational psychology at Birkbeck College: 'Employers seeking loyalty, commitment and a positive psychological contract with their employees should pay more attention to their HR policies and practices. Organizations have no excuse for a cop out that blames external circumstances for the loss of loyalty.'

While HR professionals underestimate the scale of the problem and have different views about the causes, the Sanders and Sidney report indicates a higher level of agreement between employers and employees on what could be done to improve matters.

Interestingly, neither side advocates a return to the good old days of jobs for life. Rather, both camps recognize the need for better communication in the workplace, for companies to do more to demonstrate their commitment to staff, and for greater investment in developing employees.

There is broad agreement, for example, that improved training and development programmes are one way to demonstrate employer commitment. But over 70 per cent of HR departments are keen to pass on their traditional responsibility for career management, preferring to put the onus on individuals to manage their own career development.

Commenting on the report, Sanders and Sidney's managing director Francis Cook said: 'While the research paints a somewhat bleak picture of the current situation, we were pleased to see that employers and employees believe that solutions exist. The challenge will be to find new ways of marrying the interests of the business with the needs of its people to strengthen the bonds again.'

> Talk of the disappearance of loyalty is Generation X theorizing run amok

Talk of the disappearance of loyalty is Generation X theorizing run amok. Perhaps, somewhere in California, working life really is built around a complete absence of loyalty to anything, including to any organization. Meanwhile, back in reality, many millions of people continue to work in much the same way, working much the same hours, as they have done for decades.

Sad? Some would say so. The champions of free agency would suggest that remaining with the same organization for 10, 15, maybe 20 years is mutually unsatisfactory. The employee becomes jaded, comfortable and complacent, hardly good news for any organization. The bright and ambitious new arrival is surely preferable to the cynical long-term resident with an eye on retirement and a gift for corporate manoeuvring.

The flip-side of this is that an organization populated by people whose loyalty is at best fleeting and at worst elsewhere is hardly likely to take the world by storm. Indeed, it is more likely to be riven with political intrigue, uncertainty and insecurity. Short-term employees have eyes only for the short term; free agents are set on their individual freedom and success rather than team goals. 'Mercenaries tend to move on and not become marines. Can you build a company with a mercenary force?' asks Sumantra Ghoshal of London Business School, co-author of *The Individualized Corporation*.[99]

> The bright and ambitious new arrival is surely preferable to the cynical long-term resident with an eye on retirement and a gift for corporate manoeuvring

Luckily perhaps, the talk of an army of mercenaries appears overblown. 'At its worst the free-agency argument is extremism. We exist in a trading environment. Companies trade flexible hours, decent pay, and working with colleagues, for our loyalty,' says Brian Baxter, senior partner at organizational development consultants Kiddy and Partners.

Research by Incomes Data Services found that in 1993 36 per cent of men had been with the same employer for ten years or more. This was at the peak of downsizing mania. Interestingly, and surprisingly given the hysterical talk of the emerging promiscuous workforce, in 1968 37.7 per cent of men had been with the same employer for ten years or more.

More research from Business Strategies forecast that 79.2 per cent of all employees would be in full-time permanent jobs in 2005 – compared with 83.9 per cent in 1986. The revolution has been postponed.

For better or worse, people stick around. Even after downsizing, the flurry of demographic time bombs and talk of Generation X, working life retains a strong element of security. It may be unfashionable to spend 30 years working for a single employer but many people do. Some undoubtedly do so because they have limited opportunities elsewhere, limited ambition or limited abilities. These are facts of life generally ignored by the free-agent propagandists.

But many choose to stay. Gen e are not all creating businesses from scratch; they are also reinventing businesses from the inside. (Witness our earlier examples of dual careering.) They choose to do so presumably because they find their work and working environment stimulating, rewarding or enjoyable. Indeed, some of the corporate titans of our age are devoted company loyalists. Perhaps the best known is GE's Jack Welch. Fêted far and wide as the very model of the modern CEO, Welch joined the company in 1960. No one suggests that his loyalty has been misplaced.

> Gen e are not all creating businesses from scratch; they are also reinventing businesses from the inside

With nearly forty years of service, people like Jack Welch may appear to some as a throwback to a more naïve, even simplistic age. It was never meant to be like that. In the 1970s pundits envisaged the leisure age; in the 1980s they talked of flexible working, a world of teleworkers. Well, the technology now exists and teleworking remains a decidedly minority pursuit. 'The failure of teleworking to really catch on, despite the availability of the technology, demonstrates that some sort of a physical relationship is important to people at work. People want to feel part of a team and of something much bigger. They want to be connected,' says Gerry Griffin, director of global PR firm Burson-Marsteller and author of *The Power Game*.[100]

Corporate loyalty is engendered by the fact that conventional working life still holds a remarkable attraction. Its immediacy makes business sense. In business, being there remains of crucial importance. 'The psychological dynamics of business mean that conversations in corridors or over coffee actually move the business forward,' says Brian Baxter.

The point is developed by consultant psychologist Robert Sharrock of YSC. 'A lot of people are motivated by their social needs and many also like to compartmentalize their home and working lives,' says Sharrock. 'Perhaps more important is the need managers often have to feel that they are managing. Managers make an impact, make a difference and get results by talking to people, walking around and listening to people. They need to be there and for people to be there.'

The reality is that people are loyal to the environment they spend every day in and to their colleagues. 'What corporate life can offer are the benefits of any good community – support, direction and exchanges of ideas and solutions,' says Richard Stagg, editor-in-chief for business books at publisher Financial Times Prentice Hall. 'With the right culture, the right structure and the right people, it's easy to behave entrepreneurially within the corporate universe. You can draw on the company's resources and wisdom, while moving quickly all the time. The trouble is most corporations tend towards sluggishness, trading creativity and risk for conformity and control. That's when independence beckons.'

While the traditional attractions of office life remain, it is true that companies no longer have an aura of permanence. They change with accelerating regularity. 'The profusion of joint ventures, mergers and acquisitions means that people's roles now change more regularly. In the past, people might have filled two or three roles in 15 years with a company. Now, they are likely to change every three years or so,' says Michael Greenspan of Kiddy and Partners. This, perversely perhaps, can actually encourage people to stay. If you want a fast moving, stimulating, constantly changing environment, why move when it is happening all

> Blind loyalty is undoubtedly dead – and corporate man is now as likely to be corporate woman

around you and you're a player in making it work? If you stay with a company for ten years or more, change will happen. You either develop your own skills and move forward with the organization or you leave.

All this is not to say that the corporate man of the 1950s and 1960s is alive and well. Blind loyalty is undoubtedly dead – and corporate man is now as likely to be corporate woman. 'Passive obedience was once mistaken for loyalty. The entire notion of loyalty was wrapped up with control. Now, people are not loyal in a slavish sense,' says Brian Baxter. 'This is based on the realization that you can question the system without being disloyal.'

Professor Peter Herriot, associate director of the Institute for Employment Studies, agrees that rebuilding loyalty is important, but not necessarily in the way it was once understood. 'If you mean loyalty in the sense of staying with one employer, then that is less important now, and probably not even desirable. But loyalty in the sense of trust between employer and employee is probably the major requirement underpinning today's employment relationship. Most companies rely on staff going the extra mile to deliver quality to customers. That sort of loyalty has to be a mutually reciprocal arrangement,' he says. 'The willingness of staff to go beyond the explicit terms of their contract underpins most of the management initiatives of recent years.'

What companies should not do, says Professor Herriot, is to carry

> Gen e are more questioning and demanding

on rolling out initiative after initiative with statements of values or visions which employees do not believe in. Rather, he says, they should 'make a few explicit agreements with their employees and move heaven and earth to keep their side of the bargain'.

Gen e are more questioning and demanding. They are loyal but confident enough to air their concerns, grievances and aspirations. If they were customers, we would call them sophisticated. (It is perhaps significant that we tend not to.) 'People are now more likely to question the action behind the corporate rhetoric. As a result the HR and internal communications functions are much more

> Loyalty is not dead; it simply must be earned and, increasingly, earned in different ways

important,' says Burson-Marsteller's Gerry Griffin. Indeed, internal communication has emerged as an industry in its own right, reflecting the need for companies to create communication channels with their own people.

All of this is not to suggest that corporations are workplace nirvana. A healthy strain of skepticism is evident among those who spend their lives within corporations. 'It helps to have the power of a big brand behind you and, of course, there's always unlimited coffee, fax paper and internet access,' says one manager. 'Corporations can be good places in which to learn skills, make mistakes, discover talents, build networks and identify the right personal or market niche before doing your own thing.' Loyalty is not dead; it simply must be earned and, increasingly, earned in different ways.

Figure 42.1 | Six drivers for the future[101]

Based upon the researches over the past five years of the Open University's Futures Observatory, the following have emerged as the key forces shaping the future of society over the next quarter of a century:[102]

Individual Empowerment

Although this is a slow, and often almost invisible process, it is the most wide ranging, and radical, force at work. Its main elements are:

- *Woman's Century* – many of the leaders of the new revolution will come from this 'oppressed' majority! They are, in any case, better qualified to work in the new information society, and to provide the more caring management leadership now demanded.

- *Different Forms of Family* – the new, extended family forms which are emerging from the breakdown of the nuclear family model will offer many women sole ownership of the family, but – more widely – there will be a focus on smaller communities rather than nation states (and this may lead to conflict).

- *New Politics* – the decline of political parties will continue at an accelerated pace. The ill-understood growth of a real appreciation – by people in general – that they have the right to determine their own destinies will be crucial. This has been evidenced by the growth in consumer power, and will extend to the replacement of political parties, which no longer match the aspirations of individuals, with something else – perhaps single issue parties?

- *New Values and Search for Meaning* – the move to individual empowerment will generate the need for a comparable shift in values – putting the position of society (and its social values) into a new perspective. The emerging reality of personal fulfilment will equally stimulate the search for new meaning in life, which both marketers and employers will have to address.

Symbiosis with Computer

This, as yet little appreciated, aspect will be the most revolutionary outcome of the PC revolution:

- *Personal Evolution Complements Social Evolution* – over recent history it has been society which has been evolving, but now – especially with a form of symbiosis with the

▶

networks emerging (perhaps even as 'chips in the brain') – we can also see a real possibility of an evolving form of human being; one which also lives much longer, is genetically modified to combat disease, regularly uses performance enhancing drugs, etc.

- *Communications Age* – this will eventually lead to a genuinely global village. At last, through the internet, and its future developments, we can live in a fully integrated world. The e-commerce revolution will, though, go much further than buying across the internet; to a position where 'the medium is the product'.

- *Homeworking* – the emerging technology may be significant enough for this idea to live up to its long-promised benefits, with major implications (in terms of house design) for the construction industry, and – boosted by travel taxes – may even limit the growth of the car.

- *Disappearing Computers and Mobile Communication* – with reducing costs, computing power will be incorporated where it is needed – running everything, but transparent to users – and will follow the individual, rather than be tied to a location.

Ageing

Although this is seen, by the alarmists, as a problem, it may turn out to be highly beneficial (not least for those of us who will live healthily for longer):

- *Medical Technology* – will enable chronic illness – rather than acute crisis management – to become the focus, resulting in the healthily ageing population.

- *Demography* – so, coupled with declining birth rates worldwide, the balance of the population will shift from the young to the old, potentially posing problems in the funding of welfare, though this should be readily rectified by increases in the age of retirement.

- *Employees as Customers* – the demographic changes, and the booming demands of the knowledge society, will though lead to a skills shortage. The resulting need to recruit older (previously retired?) members of the working population will turn the labour market on its head, with these employees becoming in effect 'customers', who the organizations will have to 'sell' to – not least by designing working conditions which are attractive to them (and thence to younger staff).

LLL (Life-Long Learning)

Much has been hyped in this area and little has been achieved but practical developments will ultimately appear:

- *CPD (Continuing Professional Development)* – at one extreme, the emerging skills shortage will in any case require extensive ongoing re-education (according to the EC of up to 90% of the working population), especially of older and already skilled staff, but this will be increasingly focused on individual fulfilment.

- *U3A (University of the Third Age)* – at the other extreme, the older cohorts – including those approaching (and already in) retirement – will take this individual focus to its logical extreme, creating informal, socially based, 'clubs' for their own further education, which will also appeal to the younger (increasingly well-educated) cohorts.

- *Generation Gap* – over the next 25 years the proportion of the older groups who have been exposed to higher education (and hence may be more open to the culture of LLL) will grow from less than 10% to more than 30% (and that of the younger groups may come to exceed 60%), with significant implications for the development of LLL.

New Economics

The knowledge society, coupled with the moves to personal empowerment, will result in revolutionary pressures – leading to totally new organizational forms and business processes, requiring substantial changes to economic theory:

- *New 'Products'* – lowest cost products are likely to be replaced by highest value knowledge communications. The resulting new economics will need to be developed to account for a society in which the role of most individuals lies in communications, not even in knowledge. The change will be not just to a 'service society', but to one where intellectual abilities are used to their full. Even so, the new 'soft' products will be built to last rather than be disposable. As an aside, towards the middle of the century preparation for space travel/colonization will become an important economic driver.

- *Knowledge* – the speed of growth will continue to increase, but the period of rapid, uncontrolled innovation will come to an end.

- *Rigid Organizational Structures Become Fluid Networking Cooperatives* – the shape of the organization will increasingly change to one with fluid boundaries, inside (with networking and self-managed teams) and outside (with new alliances), which favours cooperation – especially with its stakeholders – rather than competition. In this context, company database management will be one key to controlling the potential anarchy.

- *Network Trust* – with such complexity of offering, and with the 'net' (whatever that might

▶

become!) offering such a wide range of (largely unknown) suppliers, the most important feature will be that of 'trust' – established conventionally by branding and relationship management (supported by data-warehousing techniques), but increasingly through new, specialized intermediaries.

- *Competition* – stimulated by deregulation and tax reform, this extension of 1990s trends addresses a cashless society based on intellectual capital. It will, though, gradually be superseded by a widespread culture of cooperation.

- *Smaller Businesses Working Together in Less Formal Ways* – internet developments, with telecoms effectively free and the computer becoming invisible, will lead to massive inter-connectivity shaping ideas and ideology, and allowing small businesses to work informally together

New World Order

- *Global Groupings Replace Nation States* – we are seeing a dramatic growth in new 'global values', not least with the interventions in Kosovo and East Timor, being imposed on nation states, which no longer can maintain their absolute sovereignty. But these will be based on pan-national groupings (such as the UN and especially the EU, which has an almost messianic mission in this context) rather than nations (such as the US or Russia – which will continue their attempts to impose hegemony).

- *EU/EC (European Union/European Commission)* – indeed, the major political force, by example as much as by inherent power, will be the EU, which will take over global leadership (but not hegemony) from the US. It will, though, do this on the basis of the power of its philosophies rather than its armies or even financial muscle (though, as easily the world's largest economic power, that will also be important).

Globalization – continues its progress, giving a genuine global village where global governance – replacing the nation state (and its political parties) – allows resources to be coordinated globally.

Legitimation – the new values arising from individual empowerment will give rise to major problems of legitimation for national governments (but not the EU, which – as a new institution with few hostages to history – will find these easier to match).

managing gen e

I n an economy driven by intellectual capital, the question must then be who possesses the most in-demand knowledge. The new economy brings new heroes – and new villains. Until the 1980s, American business heroes were people like Lee Iacocca, the CEO of Chrysler – more John Wayne than Peewee Herman. But with the rise of Microsoft and Apple, a new kind of entrepreneur emerged. The era of nerd power had begun. The geeks would inherit the world. Gen e are here to collect.

> Gen e are here to collect

The pejorative use of the word 'nerd' in the 1980s was an indication of the value society attached to a certain set of characteristics and attitudes – a hangover, in fact, from earlier days when physical prowess and being down to earth were regarded as desirable attributes. That's now changed. 'Once a term of derision, the label "geek" has become a badge of honor, a mark of distinction', notes *Fast Company*'s Russ Mitchell. 'Anyone in business in any industry with any hope of thriving knows that he or she is utterly dependent on geeks – those technical wizards who create great software and the powerful hardware that runs it.'[103]

'The geeks know it, too – a fact that is reflected in the rich salaries and hefty stock options that they now command,' says Mitchell. There was a time when the geeks were grateful for a job that allowed them to indulge their passion. No longer. The gratitude has shifted. Companies prostrate themselves at the feet of the new wealth creators. What we are now experiencing is a shift in values. This is most obvious in the business world, where we are witnessing the rise and rise of the knowledge worker. The techies are running the show, and the techies are revolting (leaving to do their own thing).

The techies are running the show, and the techies are revolting

Switched on organizations are ruminating on how best to manage the geeks. If they want advice, who better to ask than Eric Schmidt, CEO of Novell. With a computer science PhD and a stint at Sun Microsystems, where he was a key developer of the Java software language, Schmidt is a fully paid up card-carrying geek himself.

Two years ago he left Sun to take the hot seat at struggling Novell. After years of mismanagement, industry insiders had all but written off the company. But under Schmidt the billion-dollar Utah-based networking software company has bounced back with an impressive turnaround.

'One of the main characteristics of geeks is that they are very truthful'

So how did he get the best from the Novell geeks? 'One of the main characteristics of geeks is that they are very truthful,' observes Schmidt. 'They are taught to think logically. If you ask engineers a precise question, they will give a precisely truthful answer. That also means that they'll only answer the question that you ask them.'

This, he says, is significant. If you want to get their best contribution, you have to ask the right questions. That's where Schmidt's own geek training came into its own.

Get to know your geek community

Other wise words from Schmidt include: Get to know your geek community. The geek stereotype suggests they lack social graces. But geeks are very sociable in their communities. They are tribal in the way they subdivide themselves – 'grey beards' are from the mainframe era; Unix people started 20 years ago; and now there's the new PC-plus-Web generation. The tribes get along well. They are united in fighting management.

Other tips are:

- Learn what your geeks are looking for – often more than just money.
- Create new ways to promote your geeks.
- Either geeks are part of the solution or they're the problem.
- The best judges of geeks are other geeks.
- Look for natural geek leaders.
- Be prepared when the geek hits the fan – projects that are going in the wrong direction need decisive action.
- Finally, keep project teams as small as possible.

> Ignore the geeks at your peril

Ignore the geeks at your peril. Manage them you must. Truth be told, managing gen e is no different from managing any other group of people. Manage them intelligently and sensitively and you will reap dividends. Manage them badly and you will reap a whirlwind.

understanding individuals

The first step must be a clearer understanding of what career success means to the individual. Not everyone aspires to be chief executive – or even a boss. Companies must find new ways to retain knowledge workers who are not interested in promotion.

searching for the best of both worlds

Sourcing a company's future executive population solely from within may be dangerous. Many companies now recognize the importance of bringing in outsiders to widen the management gene pool. At the senior level, however, an external appointment can drive a coach and horses through the succession plan lower down, especially if the incoming appointee brings in his or her own team. It is bound to send a signal that the company values external appointments above home-grown talent. Say you are in line for a top job and a new arrival steps in front of you: are you likely to stay or take your chances elsewhere?

succession planning

A succession plan can help retain key individuals and allow them to be groomed for the top jobs. But at very senior levels, nominating the crown prince in advance is likely to result in the loss of other talented managers. The alternative is an open race, which sharpens the instincts of the executives in the running and motivates them to higher levels of performance and commitment. This approach also has a downside, however, because it encourages political intrigue, with senior managers jockeying for power to the detriment of the business.

growing your own

> Some of the greatest leaders have a blind spot when it comes to making way for others

The attitude of senior managers can greatly influence the way succession is viewed by those within the organization. For some chief executives, in particular, the appointment of someone from outside to a top job is an admission of the company's failure to 'grow' its own people. The message for the next generation coming through the ranks is that their loyalty is unlikely to be rewarded. Encouraging talented young managers from below, however, doesn't always come naturally to those at the top.

quitting while ahead

The other side of succession planning at the very top involves persuading the incumbent to go before he or she passes their sell-by date. But some of the greatest leaders have a blind spot when it comes to making way for others.

planning to replace the irreplaceable

A few individuals – Bill Gates, Richard Branson and Rupert Murdoch, for example – are genuinely irreplaceable. Trouble is, they are now the four-star generals leading the battle for talent.

the value-led corporation

How do you bond with gen e? More and better glue. Central to the demanding nature of employees is the notion of values. In the past, loyalty was basically bought. Job security, gradual progression up the hierarchy and a decent salary were offered by the employer. In return, the employee offered unwavering loyalty and a hard day's work. Now, values determine loyalty. 'Every organization needs values, but a lean organization needs them even more,' GE's Jack Welch says. 'When you strip away the support systems of staffs and layers, people have to change their habits and expectations, or else the stress will just overwhelm them.'

> How do you bond with gen e? More and better glue

Among those companies which have sought to nurture a sense of values is Anglian Water. It formulated its vision and a values statement in 1998. The company's senior executives have since been travelling throughout the company to communicate directly with employees. 'Stating the values was an acknowledgement of the changing nature of our business and that we needed to change the way we worked,' says Anglian Water HR business manager Ian Plover. 'We won't and can't do anything without the support and involvement of our employees.' Plover – 23 years with the company – admits that loyalty is a question of belief. 'I believe in what we do. There is a feeling of camaraderie in doing something for the community and a level of empowerment within the company,' he says. 'Though the days of a job for life have gone, people need a feeling of safety and of being led. They need to know that their pay is fair and reasonable and that they have a say. They need to feel ownership.'

Another company that seems to have got the message is Waterstone's, the chain of booksellers. The company is unusual among retailers in that it recruits a very high number of graduates – 85 per cent of all new staff. The need to retain bright young employees has led Waterstone's to rethink its training and development packages.

Each member of staff will now take full responsibility for their own career development in what the company sees as a new deal with employees. Staff will work through their own skills and training portfolio, progressing at a pace and level set by themselves. The package also provides a range of more imaginative options for self-development, including training in leadership, decision-making and reacting to trends.

The man behind the rethink is Simon Jacobs, Waterstone's HR director. 'This is definitely about loyalty,' he says. 'We have a policy of internal appointments but it goes beyond that. We're a fast growing business and we see grooming people for management jobs as a business priority. What we're saying to new employees is "The ball's in your court; there are management positions if you want them but you control the pace of your development."'

> Values cannot be simplistically condensed into a mission statement or neatly printed on to an embossed card

The challenge for organizations is that values are more complex than mere money. Values cannot be simplistically condensed into a mission statement or neatly printed on to an embossed card. 'In the past there was a belief in one set of values. Now, in more sophisticated companies, there is an awareness that the uniqueness of the firm comes from multiple values and cultures. Previously, people's needs were interpreted as being homogeneous. Now there are flexible benefits and working arrangements and recognition that people are motivated by different things. Organizations have to understand what motivates individuals. Money and power don't work for everyone,' says Brian Baxter.

With values becoming an increasingly important aspect of loyalty and motivation, it is little wonder that companies are paying them more attention. Indeed, in the modern world, companies are crucial in identifying and developing the values which shape society. 'The corporation is a value creator in modern society. In our secular world, corporations create belief systems, values which people buy into,' says Gerry Griffin. Companies are the great institutions of our age. In the past, value systems were created by the church and the state. Now, companies have distinct and strongly defined value systems which we may – or may not – buy into. The choice is ours.

'Companies increasingly resemble tribes,' says Jonas Ridderstråle of the Stockholm School of Economics. 'Companies have to find people who share their values. Recruiting is now about finding people with the right attitude, then training them in appropriate and useful skills – rather than the reverse. We can no longer believe in the idea of bringing in smart people and brainwashing them at training camps into believing what is right.'

For the better executives clearly there is a choice. They work for companies which are in accord with their own value systems. If they don't want to work for a polluter, they will not. After all, people want to hold their heads up when they are with their peers. They don't want an embarrassed silence when they

> People want to hold their heads up when they are with their peers. They don't want an embarrassed silence when they announce who they work for

announce who they work for. 'These days we value a great mission and a great working lifestyle as much as a bigger desk and the prospect of promotion,' says publisher Richard Stagg. 'Who gets out of bed in the morning for a distant corporate objective? If a company gives real meaning to people's work, and the freedom and resources to pursue their ideas then it's a good place to be.' Values, it seems, are the new route to developing loyalty among employees.

Values build bridges between employees and company. Even national governments are taking the issue seriously: the Norwegian government recently announced an initiative to distil the country's core values. We examined a number of claims made about values:

- They engender loyalty among employees. As the balance of power begins to shift in favour of the individual knowledge worker, a crucial issue is how to recruit, retain and engage the very best staff. Could values provide a basis for a new psychological contract to replace job security?

- They provide a framework to motivate employees and devolve responsibility for decision making. Many companies have tried unsuccessfully to introduce 'empowerment'. Could values help support an empowered workforce?

- They offer fixed points of reference in a rapidly changing world, providing a degree of stability and continuity during periods of upheaval or times of corporate crisis. Moreover, it was suggested by some that aspirational values can support the actual process of change. Given that organizational change continues to figure prominently on many companies' agendas, and will do for the foreseeable future, what role can values play?

Different companies have different names for their core values. Values, beliefs, principles, 'essential and enduring tenets' – call them what you will – the point is not by what name they are known but what they are understood to mean.

Some confusion results from imprecise use of these terms. The most authoritative definition, in our view, is that of James C. Collins and Jerry I. Porras, the authors of *Built to Last*,[104] one of the most influential business books of recent years. Core values, they say, are: 'The organization's essential and enduring tenets – a small set of guiding principles; not to be confused with specific cultural or operating practices; not to be compromised for financial gain or short term expediency.'

Organizational goals (specific targets that help to realize a vision) are not values; neither are mission or purpose (the fundamental reason for existence); nor should values be confused with vision (a picture of the intended future). All these have their place in a successful company. Values, however, it could be argued, are the precursor, the foundation on which the others are built.

Values, then, run deep. They are timeless guiding principles that drive the way the company operates – everything it does – at a level that transcends tactical or even strategic objectives. The key which unlocks the power of values is interpretation. This is the missing link between the theory and the effective practice. The issue our research explores is the practical difference they make to a company.

So where do values come from? If values are to be effective, this cannot be a superficial exercise. The key is to capture what is authentically believed, not what other companies select as their values or what the outside world thinks should be the values. Charles Handy notes in *The Hungry Spirit*: 'It is inadequate to borrow beliefs. We have to work them out for ourselves.'[105] If a company comes under pressure for whatever reason, its guiding principles will only help if they are 'true' for that company.

Usually few in number – typically between three and ten – values are the essence of the company's identity, the corporate DNA. The values shout from the rooftops 'this is what our company passionately believes in'. For Disney, for example, they include 'creativity dreams and imagination' and the promulgation of 'wholesome American values'. For Hewlett-Packard it's a responsibility to the community that's important.

> Values are the essence of the company's identity, the corporate DNA

It would be much easier to dismiss the whole idea of values if they weren't found in such prominent and successful organizations. Some of the most successful companies go to amazing lengths to preserve their values:

- Merrill Lynch has its five 'Principles' engraved on plaques lining the corridors of its world headquarters.

- Johnson and Johnson has its values written down in a book – the 'Credo' – which dates back to the founding fathers of the company.

- Cadbury-Schweppes has set out the company's values in a document called the 'Character of the Company'.

● Hewlett-Packard has the H-P Way, which employees write out by hand and pin up next to the picture of their family.

These companies place their values above profit maximization. Yet research suggests that they outperform those companies which put profits first, providing a better return to shareholders over time.

The companies identified by Collins and Porras in *Built to Last*,[106] for example, had outperformed the general stock market by a factor of 12 since 1925. All were value-driven businesses. This fact alone justifies further investigation.

To separate out the impact of values from other aspects of company performance is almost impossible. The best companies don't even try. Many of the CEOs to whom we spoke seemed unworried by their inability to measure the impact. 'You can feel it,' one CEO told us.

managing with values

I n the relentless ebb and flow of corporate history there are rare events which change things. They become benchmarks of how best to manage. Think of Henry Ford's decision to pay his workers $5 a day. Overnight the expectations of workers changed. Perceptions of fairness were transformed. Think of Johnson and Johnson's inspiringly honest and upfront reaction to the Tylenol crisis in 1982. Now, think of the textile company Malden Mills. Think back to 11 December 1995.

At that time, the business world was in the last throes of the downsizing mania which had gripped it at the beginning of the decade. Companies were still reengineering, brutally cutting out excess. The mantra of the corporate world was survival of the fittest. Little else. Business was looking increasingly one dimensional and that dimension had little to do with compassion.

On the night of Monday 11 December at around 8 o'clock a fire took hold of part of the Malden Mills Industries complex in Lawrence, Massachusetts. Twenty-four people were injured in the blaze. The company's manufacturing capabilities were substantially affected, though not completely destroyed. It was one of the biggest factory fires in New England history. Next day as the embers still smouldered, the company president, Aaron Feuerstein, said that: 'The tragedy will not derail Malden Mills' leadership position in either the local community or the world textile market.' Brave words, but ones which were largely ignored. However high the flames, a fatality-free fire in a textile factory did not hog the headlines for long.

The world began to take notice later in the same week when Feuerstein addressed 1,000 of the company's 2,400 local employees at the gym of the town's Catholic Central High School. 'At least for the next 30 days – the time might be longer – all our hourly employees will be paid their full salaries,' he said, going on to promise to build a new plant in the area. 'We will be one hundred per cent operational in 90 days,' Feuerstein proclaimed. The crowd cheered. The newspaper writers took notes and shook their heads. Brave words. Too good to be true.

> In the age of downsizers, Feuerstein's commitment to his workers appeared outdated, a quaint throwback to another era

In the age of downsizers, Feuerstein's commitment to his workers appeared outdated, a quaint throwback to another era. It also appeared to be commercially naïve, if not foolhardy. The eventual cost of keeping the Malden Mills employees on the payroll and continuing to pay their health insurance was calculated at $15 million. As Malden Mills is owned by the Feuerstein family, it was their money on the line.

To some this seemed madness – an impetuous rush of blood. The skeptics reckoned without the leadership of Feuerstein and the dedication of the company's employees – and its customers who remained loyal even when they knew they would have to wait for their deliveries.

Malden Mills was already a pretty unusual company prior to the fire. In an age of diminishing loyalty and relentless downsizing, it stood for traditional corporate values. Loyal employees worked alongside trusting management. Customer retention and employee retention both registered a staggering 95 per cent. The company looked after its own – its salaries averaged $12.50 an hour compared with the $9.50 industry average.

The company had remained steadfastly – some said foolishly – loyal to its home base. Founded in 1906, it moved to Lawrence (from Malden near Boston) in 1956 rather than following its competitors and many more textile companies in their migration down south. 'The Merrimack Valley is an area rich in textile history and skilled textile workers,' Feuerstein explained. 'When the bulk of the textile

industry left this area for cheaper labor and less stringent environmental regula-
tions elsewhere, my family made a commitment to stay.'

Malden Mills remained stoically put, a family firm with close local ties. One
generation passed on to the next. Aaron Feuerstein, the grandson of the
company's founder, began working with the company after graduating in 1947
and took charge at the beginning of the 1970s. He appeared no Jack Welch.
Feuerstein led the company into the fake fur market. This proved disastrous. By
1980 Malden Mills was in Chapter 11 bankruptcy and had to lay off workers.

The tide turned with the development of Polartec, a lightweight fleece which
proved more successful – and tasteful – than fake fur. Polartec was developed by
the company's own researchers. Its success enabled Feuerstein to re-hire all the
people he had laid off. Between 1982 and 1995, the company's revenues more
than tripled while employee numbers merely doubled. By 1995, thanks to
Polartec, Malden Mills had sales of over $400 million.

Then the fire. Feuerstein's choice, put in geographical terms, was Florida and
retirement in the sun carrying a large insurance cheque or a cash-strapped chilly
winter in Lawrence with limited production facilities and hefty overheads. No
choice. Malden Mills was back to virtually full capacity within 90 days. It was a true
team effort – and a family one with Louise Feuerstein, Aaron's wife, playing a
leading role. Less than a year later, the company dedicated a new $120 million
plant on the site of the fire and all but a handful of employees returned to work.

'He was 70 years old and could have easily taken the insurance money and
retired comfortably and left his employees and the town of Lawrence, Mass out in
the cold. But he made what he considered the only right and ethical decision that
appeared like bad business at the time even though it was highly moral,' says
Charles Manz of the University of Massachusetts' School of Management and
author of *The Leadership Wisdom of Jesus*.[107]

'Most people would've been happy at their seventieth birthday to take the
insurance money and go to Florida, but I don't want to do that,' Feuerstein said.
'Fifty years ago it would have been considered very natural for a CEO, if his plant
burned down, to rebuild it and to worry about his people,' he lamented. 'There's

some kind of crazy belief that if you discard the responsibility to your country, to your city, to your community, to your workers, and think only of the immediate profit, somehow not only your company will prosper but the entire economy will prosper as a result and I think it's dead wrong.'

In fact, Feuerstein's chutzpah in backing his beliefs with money was commercially and financially astute. The decision to stay and rebuild attracted huge media attention. President Clinton invited Feuerstein to his State of the Union address. Universities formed an orderly queue to award Feuerstein with honours. Case studies were written for courses on business ethics. Little wonder then that insurance companies, financiers and customers responded to Feuerstein's call to arms. If they had moved slowly or unenthusiastically, the publicity would hardly have been positive. They jumped.

> Commentators, consultants and academics are hungry for matrices and complex concepts rather than old-fashioned notions

Amid the media hubhub and bandwagon boarding, the lessons of Malden Mills are easily overlooked. Indeed, their very simplicity means that this is even more tempting. Commentators, consultants and academics are hungry for matrices and complex concepts rather than old-fashioned notions. Aaron Feuerstein showed that values can allow a business to overcome apparently insurmountable obstacles.

Lesson one from Malden Mills, therefore, is that clearly defined corporate values can play an important role in the success of a business by engaging the energy, enthusiasm – and loyalty – of employees. Recent years have seen a growth in interest in the entire notion of corporate values. Malden Mills helped ignite the debate.

In the aftermath of the fire, the committed and grateful workforce worked so well that productivity and quality shot up – before the fire 6 to 7 per cent of the company's production was 'off quality'; this reduced to 2 per cent after the fire. Feuerstein said the company's employees paid him back nearly tenfold: 'I always thought that perhaps in the long run [my employees] would return to me a quality product that would make Malden Mills continue to excel. But I never dreamed there would be any short-term advantage.'

The final lesson from Malden Mills is that however great the company, however large the media coverage, however expansive the plaudits, business is hard. No one has a divine right to succeed. After rebuilding, warm winters and market forces have meant that Malden Mills has encountered some hard times – in February 1998 it cut 300 jobs and, more recently, management numbers have been reduced – but its values remain steadfastly intact.

watch Bill

You could say that gen e all began with Bill Gates. Gates may not be everybody's favourite guy. He may not even be close. But Gates it was who started the gen e revolution. He was the first, and for the time being at least remains the most powerful, of the cyber-entrepreneurs. His significance does not lie in the amount of money he has made for himself and many others. Bill Gates is significant because he was an entrepreneurial throwback.

> Gates is a genuine gen e triumph

Think of the great CEOs of the 1970s and 1980s. This is difficult. Not many stay in the mind. Harold Geneen at ITT perhaps. Lee Iacocca at Chrysler. Various luminaries trying to fix up ailing giants such as GM and Ford. The rest slip from your mind as easily as they will be glossed over by history. Gates's essential difference is that his success is built on being entrepreneurial. He is neither a numbers man like Geneen nor an in-your-face salesman like Iacocca. Gates is a genuine gen e triumph.

Microsoft's ascendancy marked a change. Gates combined technological know-how with ferocious commercial acumen. Gates was the first of the new breed of technology entrepreneurs. He was fast. He was smart. And he was hungry. Real hungry. Before him, techies were not taken seriously as business-people. After him, they were feared.

Microsoft's technology enabled people to leave the corporate fold. More significantly, Microsoft, the upstart company run by a couple of geeks, usurped the power of one of corporate America's biggest – and seemingly untouchable – players. IBM, remember, was not just any corporation. Big Blue was widely regarded as the best oiled corporate machine in the world. 'No one ever got fired for buying IBM' was its proud boast. IBMers, in their distinctive blue suits, were held in awe. That all changed when Microsoft (and to a lesser extent Intel) emerged as the new face of business.

From the cradle of the digital revolution, a new kind of business leader was emerging. The nerds were coming and Bill Gates was leading the charge. Gates is the ultimate expression of nerd power. His own rise to fame and fortune personifies a change in the business constellation. Once unfashionable in corporate America, in the wake of the computer revolution the technical experts – or techies – have risen to prominence.

> The nerds were coming and Bill Gates was leading the charge. Gates is the ultimate expression of nerd power

The young Gates with his bottle-glass spectacles, dandruff and acne, and Allen with his long hair and shaggy beard provided Americans with a caricature of the nerds they knew at school. More significantly, for the first time corporate America's discomfort with raw intellect and technical expertise was challenged.

The prevailing myth among the business community of America was that grit, determination, luck and sheer hard graft were enough to get on in business. Brains alone were not seen as the distinguishing factor. In fact, they were sometimes seen as a handicap, especially where they were accompanied by a certain social awkwardness and eccentricity. The new computer whiz-kids flew in the face of the anti-intellectual tradition, according to Randall E. Stross. 'The vocabulary might change – eggheads in the 1950s, nerds in the 1970s – but the message is the same: brains are a liability not an asset.' Gates changed all that.

It's easy to put Microsoft's success down to one extraordinary piece of good luck – securing the contract to supply IBM with the operating system for its first PC. But there was more than just luck involved. Bill Gates recognized the significance of the deal. He knew that an operating system providing a common platform could change the history of personal computing. He worked tirelessly for more than six months to ensure that the opportunity when it came would fall to Microsoft. He gave luck a helping hand.

When Gates was preparing to pitch for the IBM contract he is said to have told his mother that she would not see him for six months. During this time he virtually lived at the office devoting himself entirely to winning the IBM business. He sensed how important it was. That's the focus that gen e have inherited.

The question was whether Gates could go the distance (the same question now being asked about Jeff Bezos and the leading gen e revolutionaries). By the mid-1980s, few doubted that he was one of the most talented techies to emerge from the maelstrom. His competitive spirit and personal drive to succeed were legendary. What critics questioned were his managerial credentials. They asked whether he had the necessary skills and charisma to lead a company that was fast becoming a major player in corporate America.

As early as 1984, *Fortune* magazine chided him for failing to develop the management depth to turn the temporary victories he had won into long term dominance.[108]

Clearly, Gates has looked less sure footed of late. Leaving his legal problems on one side, dark clouds were already gathering over Redmond in the mid-1990s. Prophets of doom were predicting that the internet could be Microsoft's undoing. Gates, they said, had been caught napping by the rapid advance of the internet and how it would transform the PC software industry. Some even drew parallels with IBM, which lost its way.

A decade and a half later, the wheel appeared to have come full circle. Critics argued that Microsoft's illustrious leader was the last person at Microsoft to see the potential of the internet for home users. This could have cost the company dearly. But fortunately, when the penny finally dropped for Bill, Microsoft had the resources at his disposal to play some serious catch-up. 'The internet is not a fad in any way. It is a fantastic thing; it makes software and computers more relevant.'[109] Gates fans say this actually shows great strength of character, and is characteristic of the sort of leadership demanded in the modern business world. We all get it wrong. Gen e hold up their hands and get on with the next project, the next business.

Gates's continuing identification with gen e is summed up by a single comment: 'Size works against excellence. Even if we are a big company, we cannot think like a big company or we are dead.' True Bill.

> We all get it wrong. Gen e hold up their hands and get on with the next project, the next business

e pig

So, where can we look for inspiration? Which company manages to encapsulate the values of gen e? Well, we have talked to many and the one we keep coming back to is based in Tipton, Pennsylvania. Call them up and, as you wait to be put through, you won't be listening to the three tenors or some other classical selection. 'Kiss a pig, hug a swine, some of them are good friends of mine. I'm specifically prone to Hampshire porkers …' Not Elgar or Mozart, but Ray Stevens's 'Kiss a pig'. If you're lucky, as you approach the third verse, Ray may be cut off in his porcine prime. 'Welcome to New Pig,' says company president and CEO Nino Vella. 'Do you like the music?'

Whatever your views on the relative merits of Mozart and Ray Stevens, the New Pig Corporation has to be taken seriously – with over 300 employees and 1998 sales of $77 million, New Pig is continuing to grow at a healthy annual rate of 10 per cent. But not that seriously. After all, its cafeteria for employees is called the Pig Trough and its catalogue is known to one and all as the Pigalog. Chairman and co-founder Ben Stapelfeld simply observes: 'There is not a market in the world where people don't like to laugh and have fun or be treated as important customers.'

Fun is on the agenda and has been since the very start of the company in 1985. Back then, co-founder Stapelfeld dismissed the expensive advice of agencies and consultants and cheerfully departed to register the company's name as the Pig Corporation. He found that a Pennsylvania farmer had got there first. Stapelfeld compromised with New Pig.

Contrary to what you might think, New Pig is not some ad agency with a slick line in irony. It makes things which are neither sexy nor particularly amusing. Its products – things like absorbent socks and mats – do the industrial dirty work, cleaning up leaks and spills in factories and elsewhere. If there is a mess, New Pig wants to be there. The original idea for the pig came from an absorbent sock which wallowed in grease and slime in a pig-like manner.

To each unheralded product, New Pig brings the Pig brand. Take a typical New Pig product: a mat which can be put around a machine to soak up spills. In New Pig's hands the humble mat is reincarnated as the Ham-O PIG Mat. It comes with a colourful piggy pattern; an array of persuasive slogans – 'Scuff-resistant top layer is tough as a pig's hide!' – and a cartoon pig (dressed in piggy pattern clothes). Dull products are made fun – witness the Drain Snout and the Pig Mat. New for 1998 was the Hoofmark line of industrial cleaning products. New Pig has branded the unbrandable; it also demonstrates how gen e values and behaviour can inculcate an entire organization, anywhere, doing anything.

New Pig is a classic story of an entrepreneurial company which has – despite its name – managed to stay fresh while growing rapidly. Beginning is easy, says Ben Stapelfeld: 'You start off with zero sales. At that time, you don't think how big your market is. You want to sell something to make some money.' New Pig's absorbents and cleaning products invented a market and the company grew at 30 to 40 per cent a year. In 1990 it was rated in the top 100 of the fastest growing small companies in the USA. Sales grew by 3,595 per cent between 1985 and 1989.

'Life was wonderful but we were too busy doing what we needed to do rather than thinking about what we should be doing. We were working hard but not being that smart,' says Stapelfeld. 'It took us a long time to realize that we were a big player in a $250 million market.' The unacknowledged trouble was that New Pig's market was in fast declining manufacturing. New Pig Mark One had got as far as it could go. It had to move on to the next stage.

The trouble at this point is usually that the company founders find it difficult either to let go or to develop the new skills necessary to run a bigger company. The other original founder departed. Ben Stapelfeld set about moving the company forward.

Key to this was the realization that he and the company's management would have to change. Change, Stapelfeld acknowledged, started with him. He had to bring in some professional systems and support. 'I read a book which said that if you needed someone at level B, hire at level A,' he recalls. 'I needed a controller in accounting so I hired a CFO and paid him more than I was paying myself.' Nino Vella joined as CFO in 1986 and became CEO in 1990. Since 1990, New Pig's annual sales have grown from $13 million to over $75 million.

Vella and Stapelfeld now work in tandem as champions of change. 'We have to keep changing. That's the key job for Nino and me. We have to build an organization which embraces change,' says Stapelfeld with the air of a convert.

Change means that uncertainty and ambiguity are part and parcel of their job descriptions. 'I don't know what my job is. I'm amazed people still want me around. If you're managing properly, if you disappear you wouldn't be missed,' says Stapelfeld – perhaps the first chairman ever to celebrate the possibility of his redundancy. 'I'm the chairman but that's not more important than someone handling customer service or developing products. I still add value in lots of areas. I have ideas which are implemented and which make us money. I have fairly sound judgement for the size of business we are.'

Nino Vella is similarly candid: 'I have spent ten years learning how to run a business. It is a hard way to learn but we are all learning as we go.' How does he see his job? He shrugs: 'I'm trying to figure it out. It is best not to define yourself but to play the role necessary for the situation, issue or stage of corporate development. I look for areas where people are struggling and then support them. My role is to push the company to the next level. I have to be aware of the view from

35,000 feet – the vision – but then be prepared to go in and link what people are doing to the vision.'

Change is constant. New Pig is in the habit of questioning the basics of what it does. Take customer service. New Pig has an apparently good record. 'Right from the start we defined customer service, warehousing, fulfillment and MIS as functions that supported marketing and the customer, not necessarily finance or operations,' says Nino Vella. New Pig offers things like same-day shipping and, against conventional wisdom, keeps a massive inventory of 99 per cent of its goods because that's what customers want – even though it costs over $300,000 every year to do so. Customers are canvassed for ideas on their leak and spillage problems and how they might be solved. An impressive 10 per cent of the 5 million customers who receive the catalogue send in Dear Flabby pre-paid cards with their ideas. One bright customer idea created over $1 million in first year sales.

This was not enough. 'We are now focusing on building the company around our biggest customers,' says Nino Vella. 'To do so means that we have to change our culture. We previously believed that all customers should be handled in the same way. Now we recognize that customers are different.'

This recognition came as a shock, explains Ben Stapelfeld: 'We thought we were very good at customer service. But we brought in consultants and they said we weren't. We were very good at measuring various aspects of our performance – how many times the phones rang before they were answered, how quickly we got products to customers. The trouble was we weren't actually listening to what was important to them. We had an inside-out focus. Now we're going outside in. It is a huge change. In the past we would have a mail plan and then developed our marketing around it. Now we visit customers. In the past the only things visiting customers were catalogues.' New Pig has invested over $1 million in MIS which ensure it connects with individuals rather than plants. The new emphasis is on 'soft information', knowing more about the buying habits of individual customers.

Changing the way the company is run also means allowing others to take risks. 'One day four young guys turned up in Nino's office and said they wanted to do something else,' says Stapelfeld. 'They were smart guys who we were probably going to lose if we didn't give them an opportunity. We gave them a chance to develop a consumer catalogue. It's a market in which most people give us a very little chance of succeeding. So we've taken a chance. We gave them a budget and let them get on with it. We probably left them alone too much – you have to learn the difference between abdication and support.'

> That's the key to gen e: change the definition of what you are, today and tomorrow

The consumer catalogue was an attempt to move the company into the household products market – worth around $10 billion – where New Pig initially aims for sales of over $10 million in five years. This is part of a reinvention of the company's business. After over a decade, Ben Stapelfeld is still thinking Pig: 'We're about keeping plants clean. That's a huge market not a $250 million one. We are changing the definition of what we are.' And, finally, that's it. That's the key to gen e: change the definition of what you are, today and tomorrow.

| Figure 47.1 | **Change the New Pig way** |

- *Change starts at the top.* Says Ben Stapelfeld: 'If New Pig was only as good as me, we'd be a $10 million a year business. I am part of it and I hope a good part.'

- *Hire communicators and people willing to embrace new ideas.* 'I try to surround myself with people I can communicate with,' says Nino Vella. 'As CEO you need to engage with people's issues and problems. You have to feel the pulse of the business.'

- *Be prepared to make mistakes.* 'We can't be protected because of our positions. We have to do things and fail right there in front of everyone. That's hard,' Stapelfeld admits.

- *Forget everything you have ever learned.* 'To run a company you need to get rid of your preconceived notions. Forget them and start over,' advises Stapelfeld. 'Don't listen to what I say or what some guru says, just enjoy getting it right for yourself.'

- *Keep on learning.* 'Hell, I don't know; I'm still learning,' says Nino Vella. 'The days of running a business by a formula are past. You have to learn continually.'

- *Be upfront.* Vella and Stapelfeld talk of change constantly, but keep their trotters firmly on terra firma. Homespun, disarming honesty is part of the New Pig culture. 'Being honest is key. We don't try to manipulate things and are constantly trying not to have hidden agendas or motives. If someone thinks I am wrong they can argue with me to convince me I am wrong,' says Stapelfeld. 'People see we are vulnerable, open and honest. We are consistent so people think it is okay to be vulnerable and fail. We get things wrong a lot of the time. We just hope to have the right answer over 50 per cent of the time.'

1 Author interview.

2 *Fortune* (1999) 27 September.

3 Perkins, Anthony B. (1999) 'Greed and lack of management plague our new economy', *Red Herring*, December.

4 O'Connell, Brian (1999) 'Generation entrepreneur is rewriting the rules of business; you can too!', *Entrepreneur Media*, October.

5 PricewaterhouseCoopers (1999) *Competing in the Internet Age*, PricewaterhouseCoopers.

6 Hamel, Gary (1999) 'Bringing Silicon Valley inside', *Harvard Business Review*, September–October.

7 *Business 2.0* (1999) August.

8 O'Connell, Brian (1999) 'Generation entrepreneur is rewriting the rules of business; you can too!', *Entrepreneur Media*, October.

9 *Business Week* (1999) 15 February.

10 Tulgan, Bruce (1998) *Work This Way*, Oxford, Capstone.

11 Booker, Katrina (1999) 'Amazon vs. everybody', *Fortune*, 8 November.

12 Quittner, Joshua (1999) 'An eye on the future', *Time*, 27 December.

13 Krantz, Michael (1999) 'Cruising inside Amazon', *Time*, 27 December.

14 *Oxford English Reference Dictionary*, 2nd edn, Oxford, Oxford University Press.

15 Vries, M. Kets de and Dick, R. (1995) *Branson's Virgin: The Coming of Age of a Counter-Cultural Enterprise*, Fontainebleau, INSEAD.

16 Tillier, A. (1995) 'A fresh wind blows in Finnish business', *European,* 5–11 October.

17 White, L. (1995) 'Net prophet', *Sunday Times*, 12 November.

18 Kurtzman, Joel (1999) 'The new age of business plans', *Fortune*, 27 September.

19 'When the bloat comes in' (1993) *The Economist*, 2 October.

20 Powell, C. (with Persico, J.) (1995) *My American Journey*, New York, Random House.

21 Quittner, Joshua (1999) 'An eye on the future', *Time*, 27 December.

22 Advertisement in *Fortune* 18 September (1995).

23 Jackson, Tim (1995) *Virgin King* New York, HarperCollins.

24 Mitchell, Alan (1995) 'Leadership by Richard Branson', Amrop International

25 Peters, Tom (1992) *Liberation Management*, New York, Alfred P. Knopf.

26 Kay, John (1995) 'Is there a competitive advantage of nations?', *Siemens Review*, 5.

27 Nordström, Kjell and Ridderstråle, Jonas (2000) *Funky Business*, London, Pearson Education.

28 *Financial Times* (1998) 16 November.

29 Goleman, Daniel (1995) *Emotional Intelligence*, Bantam Books.

30 Goleman, Daniel (1998) *Working with Emotional Intelligence*, Bantam Doubleday Dell.

31 Author interview.

32 PricewaterhouseCoopers (1999), *Competing in the Internet Age*, PricewaterhouseCoopers.

33 Schendler, Brent (1995) 'Bill Gates and Paul Allen talk', *Fortune*, 2 October.

34 Collins, James C. and Porras, Jerry I. (1994) *Built to Last*, New York, Harper Business.

35 de Geus, Arie (1997) *The Living Company*, Boston, Harvard Business School Press.

36 Kleiner, Art and Roth, George (1997) 'How to make experience your company's best teacher', *Harvard Business Review*, September–October.

37 Jager, Rama D. and Ortiz, Rafael (1997) *In the Company of Giants*, New York, McGraw-Hill.

38 Johnson, Lance (1999) *Key Indicators of the Labour Market 1999*, Geneva, ILO Publications.

39 Rubin, Harriet (1998) 'Success and excess', *Fast Company*, 18 October.

40 Institute of Management (1999) *1999 Quality of Working Life Report*, London, Institute of Management.

41 Hall, David (1999) *In the Company of Heroes*, London, Kogan Page.

42 Author interview.

43 Griffin, Gerry (1999) *.Con*, London, Suntop Media; (1999) *The Power Game*, Oxford, Capstone.

44 Author interview.

45 Huey, J. (1995) 'Eisner explains everything', *Fortune*, 17 April.

46 White, L. (1995) 'Net prophet', *Sunday Times*, 12 November.

47 Author interview.

48 Kleiner, K. (1995) 'Beware experts carrying stigmas', *New Scientist*, 21 October.

49 Sahlman, William (1999) 'The new economy is stronger than you think', *Harvard Business Review*, November–December.

50 Cramer, James, 'The top 10 internet myths', www.thestreet.com/comment/wrongtactics/786636.html

51 Slywotzky, Adrian (1999) 'How digital is your company?', *Fast Company*, February.

52 Author interview.

53 Author interview.

54 Author interview. Cohan, Peter S. (1999) *Net Profit*, San Francisco, Jossey-Bass.

55 Hamel, Gary and Prahalad, C.K. (1994) *Competing for the Future*, Cambridge M.A., Harvard University Press.

56 Fingleton, Eamonn (1999) *In Praise of Hard Industries*, Boston, Houghton Mifflin.

57 Porter, Michael (1980) *Competitive Strategy*, New York, Free Press.

58 Nordström, Kjell and Ridderstråle, Jonas (1999) *Funky Business*, London, Financial Times Prentice Hall.

59 Stewart, Thomas (1997) *Intellectual Capital*, New York, Doubleday.

60 Author interview.

61 Author interview.

62 Wallace, Paul (1999) *Agequake*, London, Nicholas Brealey.

63 Author interview.

64 McKinsey and Co. (1998) 'The war for talent', *The McKinsey Quarterly*, 3.

65 Author interview.

66 Author interview.

67 Author interview.

68 Author interview.

69 Author interview.

70 Author interview.

71 Garrison Jenn, Nancy (1999) *Executive Search in Europe*, London, EIU.

72 Author interview.

73 IDC/LINK (1996) *Success Magazine*.

74 Thank you to Gerry Griffin for this material.

75 Branson, Richard (1998) BBC *Money Programme* lecture.

76 Rodgers, Paul (1997) 'The Branson phenomenon', *Enterprise Magazine*, March–April.

77 Campbell, Andrew and Sadtler, David (1998) 'Corporate breakups', *Strategy and Business*, third quarter.

78 Virgin Group literature.

79 Leadbeater, Charles and Oakley, Kate (1999) *The Independents*, Demos/ICA.

80 Cohen, Adam (1999) 'The attic of e', *Time*, 27 December.

81 Barnard, Chester (1968) *The Functions of the Executive*, Boston, Harvard University Press.

82 Kanter, Rosabeth Moss (1977) *Men and Women of the Corporation*, New York, Basic Books.

83 Richer, Julian (1995) *The Richer Way*, London, Emap Business Publications.

84 Peters, Tom (1997) 'The brand called You', *Fast Company*, August–September.

85 Author interview.

86 Caulkin, Simon (1999) 'Beware the dot.com brain drain', *The Observer*, 24 October.

87 Winter, Jonathan and Jackson, Charles (1999) *Riding the Wave*, London, Whiteway Research.

88 Webber, Alan (1998) 'Is your job your calling?', *Fast Company*, March.

89 Davis, Stan and Meyer, Christopher (1997) *BLUR: The Speed of Change in the Connected Economy*, Oxford, Capstone.

90 Handy, Charles (1997) *The Hungry Spirit*, London, Hutchinson.

91 Pascale, Richard (1996) 'The false security of employability', *Fast Company*, April.

92 Tamkin, P. and Hillage, J. (1999) *Employability and Employers*, London, Institute for Employment Studies, IES Report 361.

93 Griffin, Gerry (1999) *The Power Game*, Oxford, Capstone.

94 Reich, Robert (1998) 'The company of the future', *Fast Company*, November.

95 Fishman, Charles (1999) 'Sanity Inc.', *Fast Company,* January.

96 de Geus, Arie (1997) *The Living Company*, Boston, Harvard Business School Press.

97 Porras, Jerry and Collins, James (1994) *Built to Last*, New York, Harper Business.

98 Sanders and Sidney (1998) *Broken Bonds*.

99 Ghoshal, Sumantra and Bartlett, Christopher (1999) *The Individualized Corporation*, New York, Harper Business.

100 Griffin, Gerry (1999) *The Power Game*, Oxford, Capstone.

101 Mercer, David (1999) *Future Revolutions*, London, Orion Business.

102 See the web site at http://oubs.open.ac.uk/future or contact d.s.mercer@open.ac.uk

103 Mitchell, Russ (1999) 'How to manage geeks', *Fast Company*, June.

104 Collins, James C. and Porras, Jerry I. (1994) *Built to Last*, New York, Harper Business.

105 Handy, Charles (1997) *The Hungry Spirit*, London, Hutchinson.

106 See note 104.

107 Manz, Charles (1999) *The Leadership Wisdom of Jesus*, San Francisco, Berrett-Koehler.

108 Stross, Randall, E. (1996) *The Microsoft Way*, Reading MA, Addison-Wesley.

109 Kehoe, Louise and Dixon, Hugo (1996) 'Fightback at the seat of power', *Financial Times*, 10 June.

The Web

www.brillscontent.com

Founded by Stephen Brill, the inside on how everybody else is reporting. Beyond spin doctoring, the magazine takes the media to task for blurring the line between informing the public and merely entertaining it or selling to it. A self-conscious anachronism which shows us how far we have travelled when it comes to the mass-market consumption of news and information.

www.drudgereport.com

'I live in the moment. I don't know what I'll be doing two weeks from now. The internet gives you the freedom to go at your own pace,' says Matt Drudge, the techno-innocent abroad and breaker, from his LA home, of story after story.

www.fastcompany.com

The magazine for its times, the bible of free agency. *Fast Company* is a must read for the legions of free agents. Its niche is clear, though becoming more crowded – the thirty-something free agent with little interest in the academic prose of the *HBR* and not corporate enough for *BusinessWeek*; someone who talks in terms of projects rather than full-time jobs.

www.funkybusiness.com

Web home to the Scandinavian funksters Kjell Nordström and Jonas Ridderstråle.

www.mgeneral.com

The brainchild of business writer Tom Brown. The 'New Ideas' website is published once a week. Now averages between 35,000 and50,000 hits per week, which translates to 1.5 to 2+ million hits per year. Invaluable insights into the big ideas and the latest outpourings from guru minds.

www.suntopmedia.com

Perhaps the media group of the future. Offers free access to the iconoclastic *exec-express* newsletter.

www.tompeters.com

The top guru of the last 20 years reinvents himself for the Web. Pow! Wow! The internet is Tom Peters' natural domain.

index

ABB, 51–52
Ageing, 214
Amazon.com, 6, 23–25
Andreessen, Marc, 6
Auction web, 165–168

Bagel street, 15–17
Barnevik, Percy, 51–52
Bezos, Jeff, 6, 13, 23–25
Black, Liam, 58–59
Branson, Richard, 46–48

Cambridge, 114–115
Capital, raising, 11–14
Career management, 179–185
Chantler, Michael, 42
Computer, symbiosis with, 213–214
Corporate giants,
    erosion in, 193–194
    turning their backs on, 11–12
Corporate legacy, 61
Corporation, valued, 223–228
CREATIVE, 60–61

Dell Corporation, 101–105

Dell, Michael, 6, 101
Dial-a-Snack, 8
Dixon, Mark, 8
Downing, Danielle, 15–17
Drudge Report, impact of, 150
Dual careering, 78
Dyson, James, 85–88

EasyJet, 153
eBay, 7–8, 165
eCareers, 169–172
Education,
    business as, 7
    importance of, 41–43
eManagers, characteristics of, 95–97
Emotional economics, 53–56
Emotional intelligence, 54–56
Empathy,
    people people, 51–52
Employability, 187–189
Enthusiasm,
    business as a calling, 45–50
Entrepreneur,
    characteristics of, 29–31
    era of 3–4

new breed of, 4
wizards of e, 5
youthful nature of, 6
Entrepreneurial experience, 183
ePig, *See* New Pig
Equilibrium, finding, 77–79
Essence, focusing on the, 33–36
Ethics,
    ownership and, 57
Euro Disney, 82
Evans, Gareth, 6–7
Executives,
    gen e, attracting, 137–140
    shortage of, 131–136
Experimentation, 81

Failure, learning from, 82–83
Fairtrade, 69–71
Furniture Online, 95–97
Furniture Resource Centre, 58–59
Future, drivers for, 213–216

Gates, Bill, 235–238
Gateway, 21
Generation e,
    managing, 217–221
Generation X, 19–21
Giel, Elwin, 8–9
Girl power, surge of, 7–8
Globalization, 216
Greenberg, Jerry, 6

Hsinchu, 117–118

Ideas, crystallizing, 34
IDEO, 194–196
Individual empowerment, 213
Individualism, rise of, 163
Intellect, driven by, 121–124

Job security, irrelevance of, 184
Joronen, Liisa, 30–31

Karlsruhe, 116

Kiam, Victor, 49
Koretz, David, 7

Lavelle, James, 8
Legitimation, 216
Life-long learning, 214–215
Loyalty factor, 207–216

Malden Mills, 229–233
Merck, 59–60
Mohsan, Tahir, 6

Netscape, development of, 6
Network Marketing International, 7
New Economics, 215–216
New Pig, 239–244
New World Order, 216
Nissen, Richard, 38–39

Omidyar, Pierre, 59
Organisational glue, 201–206
Osborne, Adam, 81
Oticon, 204–206
Oulu, 114
Outsiders paradise, 149–153
Ownership, 57

Palo Alto, 107–112
Pearl Assurance, 197–199
Power Leisure, 8–9
Power shifts, 141
Psychological contract, 170–172
Pulp fiction, 152

Recruitment firms, 141
Richer Sounds, 173–178

St. Lukes, 65–68
SAS, 202–203
Self-employment, rise of, 161–163
Silicon Valley, 107–112
Snyder, Dan, 6
SOL, 30–31
Sophia Antipolis, 115–116

Soundbites, 35
Spaghetti organisation, 205
Spin-off companies, 43
Staff retention, 181–182
Stockholm, 115
Success, secrets of, 91–93

Talent shortage, 131–136
Technology, impact of, 37–40
Tel Aviv, 116–117
Thinkers, new age, 125–129
Tulgan, Bruce, 20

US Economy,
     strength of, 99–100

Values, 60–63
     managing with, 229
Virgin brand, 46–47, 155–158

Waitt, Ted, 21
What If!, 145–147
Whitman, Meg, 7–8
Work–Life balance,
     achieving, 73–75
     changing, 161
Workforce,
     mobility of, 141–144
     transformation of, 161–164
Working communities,
     characteristics of, 202
Wright, Robert, 42